Better Homes and Gardens

Christmas

"At Christmas play
and make good cheer,
for Christmas comes
but once a year."

—Thomas Tusser (1515–1580)

Table of Contents

Spread Christmas cheer throughout your home with these jolly holiday decorating ideas.

Deck the Halls

Wreaths & Garlands

Deck your doors, walls, staircases, mantels, and more with festive holiday treatments that are a twist on the traditional.

Mark a special spot for each diner at your holiday table with cheerful chair dressings, *above*. Hang a noteworthy ornament (such as this sparkling paper bell) from a strip of tinsel garland, tie the ends of the garland to the top of the chair, and embellish with evergreen sprigs.

This gorgeous ode to snow, *left,* starts with a 21-inch plastic-foam wreath, covered with fluffy, snowlike feathers. The white foam snowballs, crystalline snowflake ornaments, and ice-blue ribbons reflect the season's beauty. Instructions are on *page 26.*

A simple bells-of-Ireland swag replaces the usual evergreens on the mantel to lighten the mood, *opposite*. White pottery holds bright red and green ornaments. Vibrant red carnation wreaths add the finishing touch to the scene. Wreath instructions are on *page 26.*

Add a pretty holiday swag to your window treatments using a large beaded garland, *left*. Drape a couple of garland strings over the curtain rod, securing them with tape on the back side of the rod. For a finishing touch—like the tassel on a drapery cord—wire elegant glass balls to the garland ends and top the balls with greenery.

Cast a warm holiday glow atop the mantelpiece with this glittering wreath, *below*. Using a large straw crafts wreath for the base, wrap a piece of wire around the top to create a hanger. Then wind a 50-count strand of white lights tightly around the wreath, positioning them so they point in all directions and securing them with floral U-shape pins. Next, cover the wreath by wrapping it with tinsel garland and securing the ends with U-shape pins, taking care to avoid the cord. Pine branches and a Christmas bow wired at the top add the festive finishing touch.

Bright green apples add life and color to this ready-made ring of evergreens. Wire small and large green apples to the wreath by poking two holes, one on each side of the stem, all the way through to the bottom of the apple. Thread green florist's wire up one hole and back down the other. Twist the wire lengths at the bottom of the apple and secure the apple to the wreath.

063 JSN

WARREN

A bells-of-Ireland garland layered atop an evergreen swag and accentuated by big red bows lends a surprising boost of color and texture to a staircase. Instructions are on *page 26*.

Turn your focal-point fireplace into a canvas of creativity by heaping mounds of fresh-cut lacy cedar branches on the mantel, flanked by two lifelike mini trees, *above*. Tuck flocked snowflakes and a snowball garland among the greenery, and wind glittery star garlands in the trees. Securely hang old ice skates in the display as a wintry twist on goodie-filled Christmas stockings.
Use vintage-style cardboard letters dusted with glitter to spell out "snow" and string them across an antique mirror.

Delicate baby's breath, twiggy white berries, and translucent skeleton leaves combine on a painted white grapevine circle to create the snowy look of this wreath, *left*. Frosted glass balls and small sheer bows scattered around the wreath dress it up for the holidays. Instructions are on *page 27.*

Shades of deep velvet blues and greens bestow a gentle beauty to this elegant wreath. Against the backdrop of folded aspidistra leaves, the ornaments and soft satin ribbon appear to capture the moonlight. Instructions begin on *page 26.*

For a twist on a traditional banister, try this garland accent. Wire double swags of green tinsel garland at intervals up the banister rail and tie on ornaments dangling from silver ribbon. To add clusters of greenery and holly, tightly wrap wire around the railing for each cluster and tuck cuttings securely beneath the wire.

One way to simplify decorating for the holidays is to use what's on hand. An old wire wastebasket filled with fruit and greenery is an unexpected, but charming front-door greeting.

Revive American colonial decorating by fashioning a wreath of fresh kumquats and evergreen leaves, *left*. Hang the wreath away from direct heat and sunlight for lasting beauty throughout, or beyond, the holiday season. Instructions are on *page 27*.

This asymmetrical mantel arrangement, *below*, allows a grapevine wreath to become the "moon" in a still life arranged with burlap-balled, live mini spruce trees and a pair of wandering reindeer. To create it, cover the mantel with loose pine branches. Tuck more into the premade wreath, along with twigs spray-painted cream. Fashion hot-glued cinnamon sticks into a country field fence. String pinecones with wire and drape them below the scene. Lastly, perch votive candles in glass holders atop overturned clay garden pots.

Breathe new life into the classic Christmas palette by posing handmade ornaments primarily of deep reds and crisp whites against an evergreen canvas. Then coordinate with beautiful packages in the same colors. Ornament instructions begin on *page 27*.

Trees & Ornaments

Christmas just wouldn't be Christmas without the tree.
Get inspired to create your own unique ornaments
with these beautiful and timeless ideas.

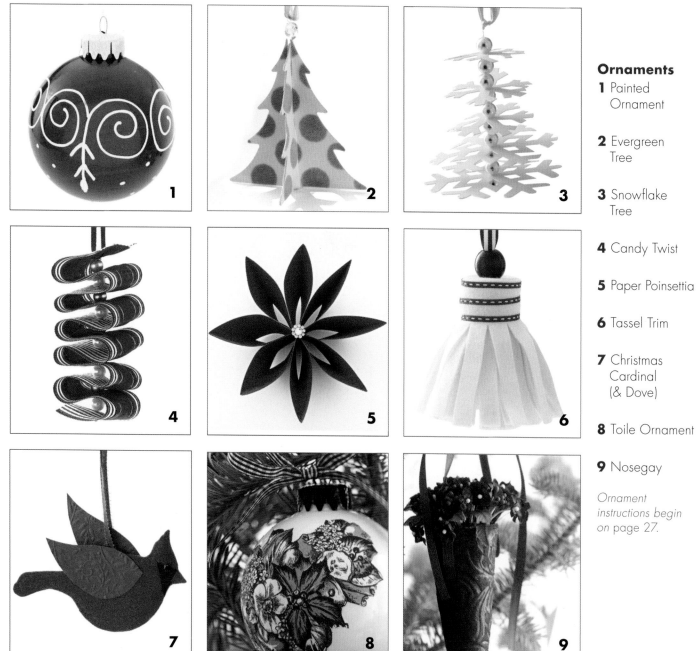

Ornaments

1 Painted Ornament

2 Evergreen Tree

3 Snowflake Tree

4 Candy Twist

5 Paper Poinsettia

6 Tassel Trim

7 Christmas Cardinal (& Dove)

8 Toile Ornament

9 Nosegay

Ornament instructions begin on page 27.

Have yourself a groovy little Christmas with this retro-inspired felted-wool ensemble, *opposite* and *above left*. The graphic design starts at floor level with a boldly dotted tree skirt and then rises to the boughs with op-art circles and triangles. Bright pink and chartreuse rev up the wow factor. The tree skirt and ornament instructions begin on *page 31*.

Each of these ornaments, *above right* and *left*, is made from three pieces of felted wool stacked and stitched together with a running stitch. Narrow silver tinsel adds sparkle to the edges.

Stockings

When Santa finally makes his entrance, he'll delight
in filling these creative stockings. Display them throughout
the house to await a Christmas eve visit.

For extraspecial gifts, white boxes from a crafts store
are tied with fabric and luxurious ribbon and then bedecked
with felt mitten "stockings," *above left*. Tuck small trinkets or
gifts inside the mittens for an additional surprise. Instructions
are on *page 33*.

No farmhouse is complete without a quilt rack, but
for a more urban attitude, paint it red and display these fun
elongated stockings, *opposite*. Instructions are on
page 33.

Vintage sweaters—too pretty to part with—get a
second lease on life when selected beading and
embroidery details are highlighted for a pair of Christmas
stockings, *above right*. Interesting buttons, once-functional
plackets, and small pockets reincarnated to hold Christmas
greenery also make each stocking unique. Instructions begin
on *page 34*.

Outdoor Decor

Delight Christmas passersby and holiday guests
with unique light shows and one-of-a-kind
displays using these bright ideas.

Strings of large frosted bulbs loop loosely around
the peaks of an evergreen garland on this fence, *opposite.*
Use one string of lights per coil and aim for loops that look
a little messy. Secure the coils with plastic cable ties and
hide extension cords in the garland.

Empty window boxes serve as bleak reminders of
warmer days. To make your window boxes as beautiful as
they were in June, simply poke evergreen branches into the
soil and wind ample lengths of glistening white lights around
them for a stunning display, *above left.*

For hard-to-reach spots, or anyplace you don't want
to use electricity, try battery-operated mini lights. Even a
bird feeder, *above right,* can be stuffed with the bright tiny
lights. There's no need for extension cords, but you may
need to replace the batteries often.

With preconfigured swags, it takes only minutes to add curb appeal, *above left*. Add a tree made from an inverted tomato plant cage. To create a finial, drill a hole in a pinecone, join the loose ends of the cage wires, and insert them into the pinecone. Top with a bow.

Put the wonders of winter to good use along a walkway or front porch. On a bed of fresh greenery, pack bundles of snow around bright red votive candles, *above right*. Make sure the tops of the votives peek through.

Use the seasonal dip in temperatures to your advantage with these handmade luminarias. Easily create each one by filling an ice-cream bucket with water, berries, greens, or other seasonal materials and freezing it. See the instructions on *page 34*.

Gazing globes once were thought to have mystical powers that brought good luck and happiness. Use oversize versions to convey your own wishes for the season. Place each globe atop an urn (smaller sizes grouped together work well, too) and accent with clusters of evergreens and red ribbon bows.

Deck the Halls Instructions

Wreaths & Garlands

Blue-and-White Snowflake Wreath

shown on page 7

MATERIALS

21-inch-diameter white plastic-foam wreath
White feather boa
Florist's U-shape pins
White plastic-foam balls: twelve 3 inches in diameter and three
   1½ inches in diameter
Spray artificial snow
10 to 12 purchased white snowflake ornaments in various sizes
Florist's wire
Ice-blue satin ribbon

INSTRUCTIONS

Cover the plastic-foam wreath with the white feather boa using florist's U-shape pins to secure. Spray white plastic-foam balls with artificial snow to resemble snowballs. Cut some snowflake ornaments in half, and tuck the ornaments' edges into the plastic-foam wreath so some of the snowflakes appear to come from various directions. Hang other ornaments flat against the wreath. Fasten the snowflakes with florist's wire. Add ice-blue satin bows to the wreath, and hang the wreath with matching ribbon.

Red Carnation Wreath

shown on page 6

MATERIALS

12- and 16-inch-diameter florist's-foam wreaths
Carnations
Small pruning shears
Red satin ribbon
Florist's wire

INSTRUCTIONS

Soak the wreath forms in water, following the manufacturer's instructions. Trim the carnations to about 3 inches. The 12-inch-diameter wreaths displayed on the mantel require about 50 carnations. The 16-inch-diameter wreath shown on the front door uses approximately 80 carnations. Insert the carnations into the form until the surface is covered (see photo 1, *above right*). Shape the ribbon into a bow (see The Bow Guide, beginning on *page 78* for bow ideas and instructions) and wrap florist's wire around the center, leaving two long wire tails (see photo 2, *above right*). Attach the bow by poking the wire ends into the bottom of the wreath. To prolong the freshness of the carnations, store the arrangements in a cool area when not in use. Artificial flowers may be used as well.

Bells-of-Ireland Garland

shown on pages 6 and 10

MATERIALS

Bells-of-Ireland stalks
Crafts wire
Ribbon
Pine boughs approximately 18 inches long

INSTRUCTIONS

Lay the bells-of-Ireland stalks on a flat work surface. Carefully wire the stalks end to end, overlapping the ends to keep the garland a uniform shape. If needed, a wire may be inserted in the stalks to provide stability. Hang as desired, and embellish with ribbon bows.

Blue-and-Green Leaf Wreath

shown on page 12

MATERIALS

16-inch-diameter plastic-foam wreath form
3 to 4 bunches of aspidistra leaves (approximately 10 leaves to
   a bunch)
Florist's U-shape pins
Round gold, blue, and green ornaments in various sizes
3 yards of blue satin ribbon
Florist's wire

INSTRUCTIONS

Separate the leaves from each bunch. Fold a leaf in half and begin to cover the wreath by securing the leaf in place with a florist's U-shape pin. Long leaves may be folded into thirds, and shorter leaves may be folded in half. Overlap the leaves around the wreath covering all areas of the wreath form.

Thread a florist's pin through the loop of each ornament and pin the ornaments between the leaves in small clusters.

Shape the ribbon into a bow (see The Bow Guide, beginning on *page 78* for ideas and instructions) and wire an ornament cluster to the center of the bow. Wire the bow with ornaments to the top of the wreath. Add a wire hanger to the back of the wreath.

Kumquat Wreath
shown on page 15

MATERIALS
12-inch-diameter metal ring
26-gauge wire
18 to 20 kumquats
Several sprigs of medium-size
   broadleaf greens (such as
   salal, photinia, or laurel)
Large-eye tapestry needle
2 yards of narrow red ribbon

INSTRUCTIONS
Secure two layers of 3- to 4-inch-long leaf sprigs to the ring, wrapping the stem ends with the continuous length of wire.

Cut a wire 6 inches longer than the circumference of the ring. Insert the wire into the tapestry needle, and thread the kumquats from side to side along the wire. Twist the wire ends together, and wire the kumquat ring to the leaf-covered one, referring to the photo, *above*. Tie the ribbon to the wreath for hanging; form a bow with the tails.

Baby's Breath Wreath
shown on page 11

MATERIALS
14-inch-diameter grapevine wreath
Cream-colored spray paint
12- or 14-inch-diameter white berry wreath
26-gauge silver wire
Wire cutters
Four or more bunches of natural white gypsophila
2-inch-diameter frosted glass bulbs (we used 16 of them)
One or two packages of off-white skeleton leaves
10-foot length of crystal-with-green-leaf-beaded garland
Glue gun and hotmelt adhesive
6 yards of ⅝-inch-wide pale green sheer ribbon
Florist's picks

INSTRUCTIONS

Spray the grapevine wreath with the cream paint; let the paint dry. Position the white berry wreath on the grapevine wreath; wire in place.

Separate the gypsophila into small bunches. Wire the small bunches around the inner edge of the berry wreath, overlapping to cover the ends. Arrange the glass bulbs on the wreath. When you're pleased with the arrangement, wire the bulbs in place. Hot-glue skeleton leaves around the wreath, filling in any open spaces and tucking the leaves between the layers.

Drape the garland around the wreath; wire in place. Make a pale green sheer ribbon bow with 10-inch-long tails. Wire the bow to a florist's pick and insert at the center top of the wreath. To make a ribbon pick, fold the sheer ribbon back and forth, creating four 2-inch-long loops on each side. Wire the center of the folded ribbon to a florist's pick and stick the pick in the wreath. Repeat to make four or five ribbon picks.

Trees & Ornaments
Painted Ornament
shown on pages 16 and 17

MATERIALS
Round red and white glass ornaments
Spray paint: red, white
Ultra-fine-point permanent marking pen
Cotton swabs
Rubbing alcohol
Plaid Tip Pen set
Dowel stick or pencil
Coffee cup or paper cup
Small items, such as marbles, to weight the cup
Folk Art Enamels Paint: #4001 Wicker White and #4006
   Engine Red

INSTRUCTIONS
Note: *Ornaments with an outer glaze or frosted matte finish are not suitable for this technique. To determine the finish on your ornament, remove the metal top and brush the exposed top of the ornament with a cotton swab dipped in alcohol. If the finish is not altered, the ornament is acceptable.*

Spray-paint the metal top white for red ornaments and red for the white ones.

Using the marking pen, mark four equally spaced dots around the neck of the ornament. Making light marks with the marking pen, follow each dot down the sides of the ornament, stopping three-quarters of the way. Use a cotton swab dipped in alcohol to erase and redraw the lines if necessary.

Referring to the photographs, randomly draw the swirls, circles, lines, dots, and squiggles with the marking pen within the quadrants.

Follow the manufacturer's instructions with the Tip Pen set to prepare the paint bottles. Use the second-largest micro tip from the set.

Prepare a drying area for your ornament by placing a dowel stick in a weighted cup.

Hold the ornament in your hand, supporting it with your thumb and fingertips, and begin painting the design. Do not touch the micro tip to the ornament; let the paint flow onto the drawn lines. Turn the ornament as you paint your way around the design. Paint the top section of the ornament first; allow it to dry on the dowel for 2 to 3 hours. Paint the bottom section in the same way. When dry, replace the metal top.

Evergreen Tree
shown on pages 16 and 17

MATERIALS
Green patterned paper
White card stock
Snowflake and tree die-cut shapes (available at scrapbooking stores)
Straightedge and crafts knife
Small hole punch
Glue gun and hotmelt adhesive
Thin monofilament line
Embroidery needle
Small green bead
Medium-width ribbon

INSTRUCTIONS
Note: *If your patterned paper is one-sided, use spray adhesive and join the wrong sides of two sheets of paper.*

Die-cut two trees from green paper and one snowflake from white card stock.

Using the punch, make a hole in the center of the snowflake.

With scissors, cut a 1½-inch slit down the center of one tree, starting at the tip of the tree. Make a 1⅛-inch slit on the center of the other tree, starting at the trunk. Slip the two trees together to form a dimensional tree.

Insert the tree trunk through the hole in the snowflake and glue the trunk sections to the bottom of the snowflake.

Thread a needle with monofilament line. Push the needle through the tip of a tree; add the bead and then sew the monofilament to the center of the ribbon and secure. Tie the ribbon in a knot to form a hanging loop.

Snowflake Tree
shown on pages 16 and 17

MATERIALS
Two 4-inch and four 2¾-inch die-cut snowflake shapes
Embroidery needle
Long-eye beading needle
White embroidery floss
Ten 10-millimeter round white pearls
Medium-width ribbon

INSTRUCTIONS
To give shape to the tree, slightly trim the tips from one large and one small snowflake shape. Use the embroidery needle to push a small hole through the center of each snowflake.

Thread the beading needle with an 18-inch length of embroidery floss. Slip a pearl onto the floss. Carefully remove the needle and then rethread it with both ends of the floss. The ends of the floss should be even.

Thread the needle through the bottom of a large snowflake; add two pearls. Thread the needle through the remaining snowflakes, from largest to smallest, adding two pearls between each shape. Finish with a pearl at the top. Sew through the center of the ribbon and secure the thread.

Candy Twist
shown on pages 16 and 17

MATERIALS
Spray adhesive
Wide, medium, and narrow ribbon
Water-soluble marking pen
Long-eye beading needle
White embroidery floss
Eleven 10-millimeter round pearls

INSTRUCTIONS
Glue the medium-width ribbon to the center of the wide ribbon. Trim the length to measure 16½ inches.

Using the pen and a ruler, mark dots down the center of the ribbon at 1½-inch intervals on both sides of the ribbon. Thread the beading needle with an 18-inch length of embroidery floss. Slip a pearl onto the floss. Carefully remove the needle, and then rethread it with both ends of the floss. The ends of the floss should be even.

Push the needle from one side of the ribbon through the other side at the first mark (the first pearl is now at the bottom of the ornament); add a pearl. Push the needle from the one side of the ribbon through to the other side at the second mark; add a pearl. Continue until you have 11 pearls on the string.

To finish, secure the thread and attach a hanging ribbon.

Paper Poinsettia

shown on pages 16 and 17

MATERIALS

Two sheets of red card stock
Straightedge and crafts knife
Double-stick tape
Glue gun and hotmelt adhesive
Rhinestone brad

INSTRUCTIONS

Cut two 6-inch squares from the red card stock.

Referring to the diagram, *right,* use a light pencil to divide one square into quadrants (this is the A side). Turn the square over; this time, divide it diagonally into quadrants (this is the B side). Draw a 1½-inch-wide border around the inside of the square, creating a smaller 3-inch square in the center. Cut out the 3-inch center, making a frame. Erase one of the lines on the A side of the frame. Repeat for the other 6-inch square. Using the straight edge and a crafts knife, lightly score along the penciled lines. Fold the lines along the scored edges. *Note:* Each frame will be folded to create one half (four petals) of the poinsettia.

Cut three ½-inch pieces of tape. Place the frame on a flat surface with the A side down and the unscored side closest to you. Place the tape next to the folds as shown on the diagram (you can place the tape on either side of the scored lines). Fold the paper along one scored line with the tape in between; repeat for the other two scored lines. As you work, let the petals fold over to the A side. Turn the shape to the A side. Using hot glue, secure the three inner points of the petals to the center of the unscored edge. One half of the poinsettia is completed.

Repeat the instructions for the other half. Glue the halves together and then use a rhinestone brad for the center.

Tassel Trim

shown on pages 16 and 17

MATERIALS

One 4½×18-inch strip each of red and dark red wool felt
   (or ivory and dark ivory)
Hanging and trim ribbons
Glue gun and hotmelt adhesive
Wooden bead

INSTRUCTIONS

Mark an 18-inch-long line 1⅛ inch from the top long edge of each felt strip. Make ½-inch cuts, starting at the bottom edge and stopping at the marked line. Stack the two felt strips, matching all the edges.

Fold the hanging ribbon in half; glue the cut ends in one corner of the felt, ½ inch down from the top edge.

Begin gluing and tightly rolling the tassel top, stopping ½ inch from the end. Wrap the top with trim, tucking and gluing the ends in place. Slip a bead over the top of the ribbon hanging loop.

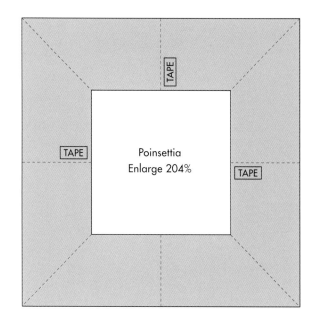

Poinsettia
Enlarge 204%

Christmas Cardinal & Dove

shown on pages 16 (cardinal and dove) and 17 (cardinal)

MATERIALS

Red or ivory wool felt
Timtex interfacing
Dark burgundy print fabric (for the cardinal only)
Red or ivory embossed paper
Double-stick fusible web
Matching sewing thread
Small beads for eyes
Narrow hanging ribbon
Glue gun and hotmelt adhesive

INSTRUCTIONS (for one dove and one cardinal)

Use the patterns on *page 30* to cut out each bird's pieces from the wool felt. Use the dotted-line patterns to cut each bird's body from the Timtex interfacing. Cut two wings for each bird from the embossed paper. For the cardinal, cut two face triangles from the print fabric.

Following the manufacturer's directions, apply fusible web to one side of the felt birds, reversing the direction of one. For the cardinal, apply fusible web to the face triangles and fuse to the bird shape.

Fold the hanging ribbon in half and place it ½ inch from the top center of the bird. Lay the interfacing shape on top and then lay the second felt bird shape on top. Carefully fuse the shapes together. Glue the wings to each side of the bird. Using thread and needle, attach the bead eyes.

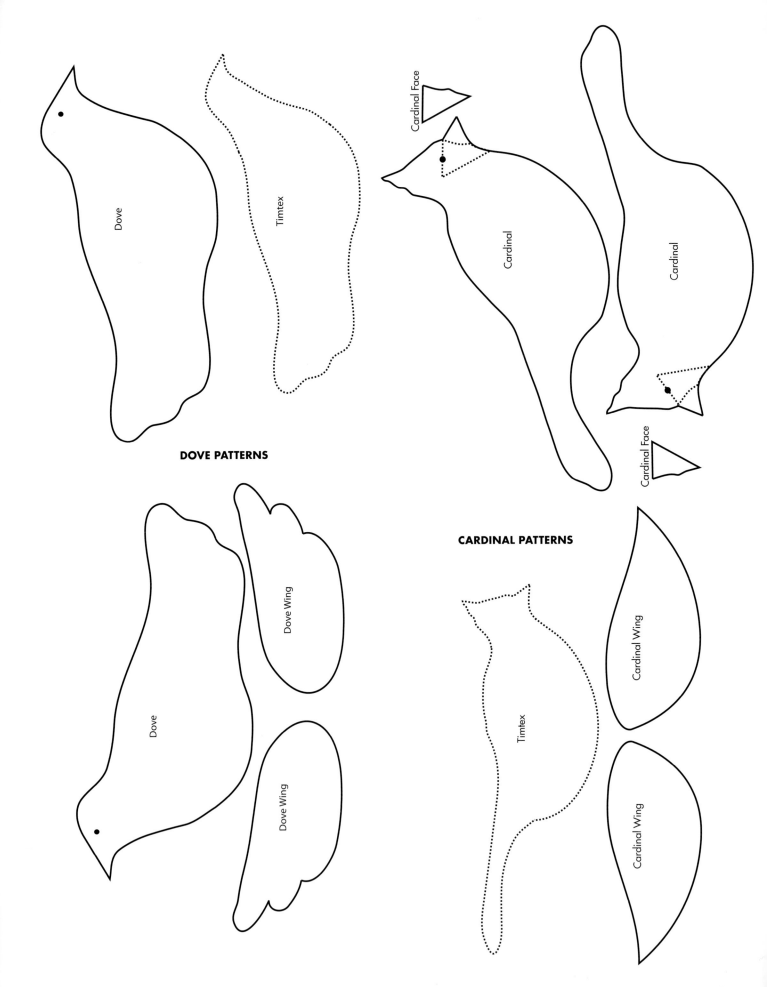

DOVE PATTERNS

Dove

Timtex

Dove

Dove Wing

Dove Wing

Cardinal Face

Cardinal

Cardinal

Cardinal Face

CARDINAL PATTERNS

Timtex

Cardinal Wing

Cardinal Wing

Toile Ornament

shown on pages 16 and 17

MATERIALS
Round ornaments
Spray paint: red, white
Medium-size drinking cups with 3-inch-diameter openings
Toile napkins
Flat artist's brush
Decoupage medium

INSTRUCTIONS
Remove the ornament tops and spray-paint some with red and others with white.

To steady the ornaments, place them top side down into the cups.

Cut out images from the napkins and lay them right side down into the palm of your hand. Brush a thin coat of decoupage medium on the image, and carefully press it onto the ornament, smoothing any wrinkles.

Allow ornaments to thoroughly dry in the cups. Replace the painted ornament tops.

Nosegay

shown on pages 16 and 17

MATERIALS
9×12-inch pieces of fusible web, red vellum paper, and red embossed felt
8-millimeter textured red pearl
Matching sewing thread
Glue gun and hotmelt adhesive
Narrow ribbon
Polyester fiberfill (optional)
Silk flowers

INSTRUCTIONS
Following the manufacturer's instructions, fuse the vellum to the wrong side of the felt. Enlarge the pattern, *above right,* with a photocopier. Using the pattern, trace and cut out one shape from the felt. Place the shape vellum side up on a flat surface. Thread the pearl on a length of thread; glue the ends to the vellum side of the shape with the pearl just below the point. Roll and glue the shape into a thin cone.

Glue hanging ribbon loops to the sides of the cone. Stuff the cone with fiberfill. Run glue around the top inside edge of the cone and insert the bouquet.

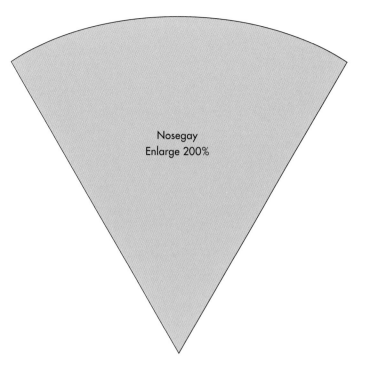

Nosegay
Enlarge 200%

Mod Tree Skirt

shown on pages 18 and 19

MATERIALS
54-inch-wide felted wool fabric: 1½ yards cream, 1 yard grass green, ¼ yard *each* of dark green and chartreuse, and ⅛ yard *each* of red, pink, and bright pink
Disappearing fabric-marking pen or pencil
1 yard of string
Three ¾×1¼-inch pieces of hook-and-loop fastener
Matching sewing threads
Silver tinsel, nonwired
Fabric adhesive

INSTRUCTIONS
Cut a 50-inch square from cream felted wool fabric or sew together fat quarters using a ¼-inch seam allowance to achieve a 50-inch square, pressing the seams open.

Fold the fabric into quarters with wrong sides facing out. Tie one end of the string to the marking pen or pencil. Pin the remaining end of the string to the folded corner of the fabric opposite the cut edges, keeping 25 inches of string between the fabric corner and the pen. Draw a partial circle on the fabric with the marking pen by making an arc with the string fully extended, as if drawing with a compass. For the tree-trunk opening, shorten the length of string between the fabric corner and pen to 3 inches; draw a second arc on the fabric. Cut through all fabric layers on the marked lines. For the center back opening, cut through one fold from the outer edge to the tree-trunk opening.

For the border, cut enough 1-inch-wide bias strips from the grass-green fabric for the inner and outer borders. Sew the short ends of the strips together with diagonal seams to make one long strip; press the seam allowances open. Align the border with the outer edge on the right side of the skirt; topstitch close to both long edges. Trim any excess strip fabric. Sew the border strip to the tree-trunk opening edge in the same way.

Cut two 1×25-inch strips from the cream fabric for the center back edges. Align a strip with each center back edge on the wrong side of the tree skirt. Sew close to each long edge and trim the excess strip. To close the skirt, sew hook-and-loop fasteners at the top, bottom, and in the center of the back edges.

Cut the following circles from felted wool: five 7-inch dark green, five 6-inch grass green, five 5-inch chartreuse, six 4-inch red, six 3½-inch pink, and seven 3½-inch bright pink.

Referring to the Assembly Diagram, *right top*, arrange the circles on the tree skirt, layering the greens from the largest to smallest and the pinks on the reds. Sew the circles to the skirt, zig-zag-stitching over the edges of each circle. Glue tinsel over the edge of each bright pink circle.

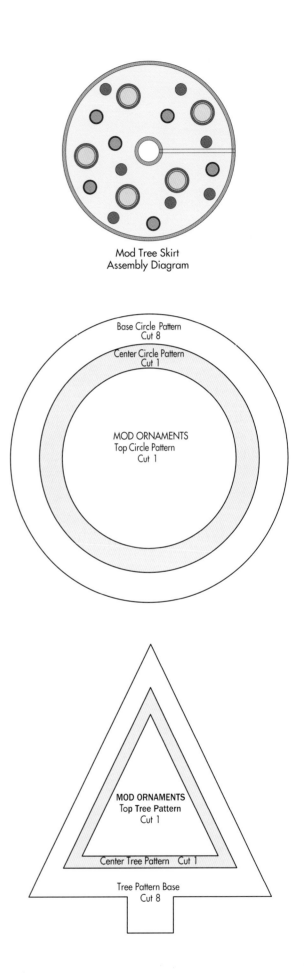

Mod Tree Skirt
Assembly Diagram

Base Circle Pattern
Cut 8

Center Circle Pattern
Cut 1

MOD ORNAMENTS
Top Circle Pattern
Cut 1

Mod Ornaments

shown on pages 18 and 19

MATERIALS
White paper
Felted wool fabric: three shades of green for the tree; red and two shades of pink for the circle
Needle and matching sewing thread
¼-inch-wide green or red satin ribbon
Fabric adhesive
Silver tinsel, nonwired
Micro-fine silver glitter
Note: Finished ornaments are approximately 3 inches tall.

INSTRUCTIONS
Trace each tree or circle pattern, *right center* and *right bottom*, onto white paper. Cut out the shapes.

Use the pattern pieces to cut eight bases, one center, and one top from the corresponding felted wool for each ornament. For the tree, use dark green for the base, medium green for the center, and light green for the top. For the ball, use red for the base, light pink for the center, and dark pink for the top.

Layer the medium and top pieces on one base. Sew the pieces in place close to the edges with small, evenly spaced running stitches. Stack the eight base pieces with the embellished one on top. For the hanging loop, cut a 5-inch length of ribbon. Fold the ribbon in half and glue the ends at the center top of the ornament between the third and fourth base pieces. Sew the base pieces together with running stitches around the perimeter of the shape. To make a running stitch pull the needle up through the fabric, insert back into the fabric about ¼ inch away, and pull the needle up close to where you inserted it down and continue in same manner.

Glue tinsel to the front and back edges of the ornament. To cover the area between the tinsel, apply a smooth layer of glue and immediately sprinkle silver glitter onto the glue. Let the glue dry.

MOD ORNAMENTS
Top Tree Pattern
Cut 1

Center Tree Pattern   Cut 1

Tree Pattern Base
Cut 8

Stockings

Farmhouse Stocking

shown on page 20

MATERIALS

Graph paper (optional)
⅞ yard each of two coordinating fabrics for stocking and lining
Matching sewing thread
½ yard of pompom trim
6-inch length of ¼-inch-wide ribbon

INSTRUCTIONS

Enlarge the Farmhouse Stocking pattern *right* using a photocopier. Cut a stocking front and back and a lining front and back. Allow for ½-inch seam allowances.

Sew the stocking front to the back, leaving the top edges open. Trim the seams and clip the curves. Turn the stocking right side out; press.

Fold the top edge of the stocking over so the lining makes a cuff. Trim the cuff with pompom fringe. For the hanging loop, fold the ribbon in half and sew the cut ends to the top inside corner of the stocking.

Felt Mitten Ornament

shown on page 21

MATERIALS

Child's mitten
Tracing paper
Red and white felt
Spray adhesive
Red and white yarn
Embroidery needle
6-inch length of ⁵⁄₁₆-inch-wide red-and-white check ribbon
Glue gun and hotmelt adhesive
Red and white buttons

INSTRUCTIONS

Trace a child's mitten to make a pattern. Use the pattern to cut four mittens from red and white felt. Glue together the four mittens in a stack with spray adhesive, aligning all the edges. Blanket-stitch the curved edges of the mittens with contrasting yarn.

For the hanging loop, fold the ribbon in half and hot-glue the cut ends to the back of the mitten.

Cut a 1¾×14-inch cuff from felt. Fold the cuff in half length-wise; spray with adhesive. Wrap the cuff around the mitten top, overlapping the short edges and hot-gluing in place. Hot-glue buttons to the mitten front.

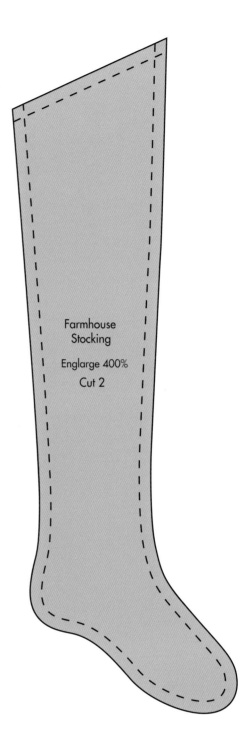

Farmhouse
Stocking

Englarge 400%
Cut 2

Sweater Stocking

shown on page 21

MATERIALS
Graph paper
Vintage beaded sweater (pullover or cardigan)
⅝ yard of sage green satin or crepe-back satin
Matching sewing thread

INSTRUCTIONS
Enlarge the stocking pattern, *opposite,* on a photocopier. Cut out the pattern piece. Sew all pieces with right sides together, using ½-inch seam allowances unless otherwise stated.

Cut the Fabric
Use the stocking pattern to cut one shape from the vintage sweater for the stocking front, positioning the pattern to utilize the beaded design and construction details such as buttons and pockets. From the remaining portion of the sweater, cut a strip 4×19 inches for the cuff, utilizing the hem or ribbing if desired. (If using ribbing as shown for the taupe-color stocking, cut the strip 1½×17 inches.) From sweater fabric, cut a 1½×6-inch strip for the hanging loop.

From the satin fabric, cut one stocking for the stocking back and two for the lining.

Sew the Stocking
Sew the stocking front to the back, leaving the top edge open. Press the seam allowances open as much as possible. Turn the stocking right side out.

Sew the lining front to the back, leaving the top edge open. Trim the seam allowances to ¼ inch. Zigzag-stitch or overcast the lining seam allowances. Slip the lining inside the stocking with wrong sides facing. Baste together the top edges of the stocking and lining.

For the hanging loop, fold in ½ inch on the long edges of the 1½×6-inch strip. Fold the strip in half lengthwise, aligning the folded edges. Machine- or hand-sew the long edges together opposite the fold. Fold the strip in half, forming the loop. Baste the ends to the top inside corner on the heel side of the stocking with the loop inside the stocking.

For the cuff, sew together the short edges of the 19-inch strip, forming a circle. Press the seam allowances open. Slip the cuff inside the stocking with the right side of the cuff facing the stocking lining, aligning the cuff seam with the heel seam and keeping the raw edges even. Sew the cuff to the stocking; press the seam allowances toward the stocking.

Edge-stitch around the stocking opening by sewing ¼ inch from the top of the stocking, through the stocking and seam-allowance layers. Turn the cuff to the outside; fold the hanging loop up toward the cuff.

For the cuff of the taupe stocking, sew together the short edges of the 17-inch strip, forming a circle. Press the seam allowances open. Slip the cuff over the stocking with the right side of the cuff facing the stocking, aligning the cuff seam with the heel seam and keeping the raw edges even. Sew the cuff to the stocking. Fold the cuff up from the stocking and press the seam allowances toward the stocking.

Outdoor Decor
Ice-Block Luminarias

shown on page 24

MATERIALS
Plastic ice-cream bucket
Berries, greenery, or other filler material
Small plastic deli-food container
Heavy stone
Heavy-gauge wire
3 to 4 yards of wide ribbon
Candle

INSTRUCTIONS
Arrange berries, greenery, or other filler material in a plastic ice-cream bucket; fill the bucket one-third full of water and freeze. Place a small plastic deli-food container in the center of the bucket atop the bottom ice layer; weight the food container with a stone or other heavy material to hold it in place. Fill the bucket with more water up to but not over the top of the center container. (If using cranberries or other floating material, fill the bucket partway, add the material, and freeze. Add more water and berries, and freeze again.)

Cut two 10-inch lengths of wire. Twist the middle portion of one wire around a pencil or dowel to create a loop for hanging. Top the bucket with more water and insert the long portions of the wire into the bucket, leaving the loop above the water. Repeat with the other wire, positioning it opposite the other loop. Freeze. Once the entire creation is frozen, rinse the outside of the bucket under warm water to remove the ice form and the center plastic container; refreeze the ice block.

Cut 1½ to 2 yards of ribbon length for each wire hook; thread ribbon through each wire loop and tie the ends over a tree branch or other hanger. Place a candle in the center space.

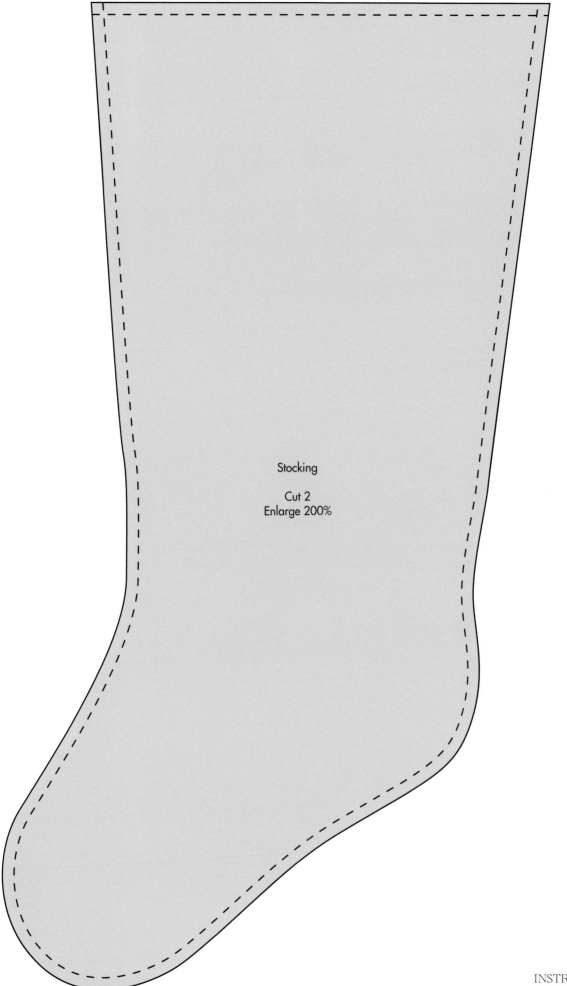

Stocking

Cut 2
Enlarge 200%

Short on time?
These quick-as-a-
Santa's-wink ideas
will add Christmas
cheer to your
holiday decor.

In a Twinkling

Beaded topiaries lend a dose of holiday spirit to a side table. These trees were made by wrapping different-size plastic-foam cones with beaded garland and then painting them to achieve a luster. A sprinkling of glitter while the paint is still wet adds extra glimmer. Instructions are on *page 58*.

Tiny Trees

If you're short on space, or are just partial to Christmas trees, these small-scale pines will fit perfectly on a shelf, mantel, or small table.

Three shades of green paint turn these paper pines, *left* and *below*, into a mighty miniature forest. Each tree gets its dimensional look by sliding flat paper pieces into a slit in the center piece. For a snow-capped look, glass glitter coats the star and boughs. A coating of green, black, and white glitter covers the interior portions of each tree. Instructions are on *page 59*.

The Tinkertoy tree, *above,* is a colorful version of a traditional feather tree with its open, stick-style branches. Simply assembled like stacking spokes in a wheel, it's a fun, unexpected decoration that you can adorn with miniature ornaments.

Playful curls lend a fanciful feel that mimics the look of a real Christmas tree, *right.* The secret is a liberal layering of fresh bay leaves.

Instructions are on *page 58.*

Put some dazzle in your decor with these sparkling, snowcapped topiaries. To make them, punch enough leaf shapes from green card stock to cover a plastic-foam cone (these are 8, 12, and 16 inches tall). Mix equal amounts of white glue and water in a bowl, and white glitter and mica flakes in another bowl. Use tweezers to dip leaves into the glue mixture and then into the glitter mixture; let dry. Starting at the base of a cone, attach the leaves with straight pins. For a natural look, avoid pinning the leaves in straight lines. Continue until the cone is covered with leaves.

Centerpieces & Table Settings

Before you sit down for your holiday dinner, set the table with a striking centerpiece and then complete the scene with a clever place setting for each guest.

Transform a footed glass serving piece into a tabletop focal point by placing a few stems of your favorite flowers into cranberries, *opposite*. To create an arrangement similar to this one, place a piece of florist's foam (fresh-flower variety) into a 10-inch-diameter bowl and then pour in cranberries. Secure about two dozen paperwhite stems into the foam and add more cranberries.

Pillar power comes from a cluster of nine identical pillar candles on a bed of fake snow, *above*. Fashion your own candle ring by surrounding the grouping with layers of twiggy branches and red hypericum berries. Finish by wrapping the arrangement with a wide velvet ribbon secured with straight pins.

A glittery beeswax bow wraps a plain pillar in holiday spirit, *right*. Display the candle on a silver pedestal with evergreen and glass ornaments for a pretty-as-a-package presentation. Instructions are on *page 60*.

These decorative balls fashioned from red, green, and white Christmas bulbs make their presence known when grouped en masse in a bowl along with a few glass-ball ornaments. Use them to form a low centerpiece that won't impede with the conversation of guests around the dinner table, *bottom left*. Or turn them into ornaments by outfitting the plastic-foam ball in which the bulbs are inserted with a ribbon for hanging.

Let there be light! With a candle tucked into a bowl of Christmas bulbs, that plea is almost a given, *bottom right*. Insert a pillar into a clear-glass footed bowl or compote and then fill the bowl with lightbulbs to hold the candle in position (for extra security, insert the candle into a candleholder before placing it in the bowl). Position bulb-filled dishes by each place setting or at evenly spaced intervals down the center of the table for easy, inexpensive table ornaments.

Fresh floral arrangements
can be pricey, but these lush
wreaths using inexpensive red
carnations are anything but.
Place a moistened florist's-foam
wreath base on a silver platter
and insert carnation stems into
the base in two layers. Insert a
small white or silver ornament
in the center of each bloom.
Add a glass hurricane lamp
and an ivory-colored candle
to each wreath.

Set a nontraditional—yet relevant—color scheme for your party, such as this loose interpretation of silver and gold, *opposite*. Display just one treasured ornament under a cloche. An upturned glass vase or compote would work as well.

Spell out a word of greeting with letters written with glue on large Christmas ornaments, *above*. Sprinkle the wet glue with glitter and shake off the excess. Place the ornaments on tall glass candlesticks.

This fire-and-ice centerpiece, *right,* is dramatic yet easy to make. Pour water into a square or rectangular watertight container, leaving enough space at the top for water displacement. Add in cranberries, rosemary, and citrus. Submerge three empty soup cans in the center of the larger container to make indentations for votives and freeze. When the centerpiece is completely frozen, fill the cans with warm water for easy removal.

Tickle each guest's sweet tooth with this lightning-fast licorice place setting. Loosely wrap a length of green grosgrain ribbon around a folded napkin, tuck in a piece of red licorice, and top it off with a small red glass ornament. Display each guest's name on a coordinating licorice easel.

Hal

Fashion playful place settings by layering red and white dishware atop large store-purchased paper snowflake mats, *above left.* Give plain bowls a temporary wintry face-lift by adding snowflakes punched from red paper and glued in place. For a peppermint twist, add festive favors like these candy canes and evergreen sprigs bound together with string.

There's no reason to splurge on fancy napkin rings when a handcrafted one can do the job just as well—and at a fraction of the cost. Fashioned from three coordinating ribbons and topped with a red Christmas bulb, this napkin ring, *above right,* offers season's greetings. Use hot glue to fasten the velvet and plaid ribbon ends together at the back. Tie the green satin ribbon around the metal part of the Christmas bulb. Another dab of hot glue attaches a sprig of greenery and holly berry to the knot of the bow.

Light up your place cards and bring smiles to your guests' faces when they sit down to dinner with these clever place cards, *right.* Place a votive in a glass mug and add coffee beans and a candy cane in the space between the two containers. Attach a ribbon and metal-rimmed name tag to the handle.

Spell out your Christmas greeting with Scrabble game tiles.
A pretty silver tray accented with complementary ornaments and
a bit of greenery finishes off this composition. Other good
options: old wooden blocks and vintage printer's letters grouped
as a centerpiece, at place settings, or in an entry.

All Around the House

You'll find something to embellish every nook 'n cranny of your home in this collection of super-simple ideas. Spruce up a chair, a tabletop, and even a window for a festive touch.

Creating pillows from purchased knit sweaters is a great introduction to the felting process that gives quick and impressive results. Embroidery lends a decorative flourish to the ski-motif pillow, *above,* and ribbing brings texture and a subtle striped design to the pillow in the background.

Use patterned sweaters to create a cozy pieced throw, *right.* Remnants of a felted reindeer sweater form the center block of this patchwork throw, and solid-color blocks ground the patterned pieces. The edges are unbound for a more casual look.

Pillow and throw instructions begin on *page 61.*

Looking for a clever alternative to the traditional front-door wreath? Add a wintry welcome to your front door with a pair of mittens filled with mixed holiday greenery, hung simply from a wide-ribbon hanger, *right*.

Make candleholders, *below,* that reflect your sparkling personality. Coat juice glasses with clear crafts glue and then bring on the shimmer by rolling the glasses in clear glitter. Use hot glue to attach silver braid trim around the glass rim, and crown your achievement by gluing on faux gems.

Dressed in wool felt hats and scarves, this snow family is ready to brave the elements—or just the toasty warmth of your home. Simple painting transforms wooden shapes, which range in height from 6½ inches to 10 inches. Rolled clay forms their carrot-shaped noses. Instructions are on *page 63.*

Your friends won't believe you made these fabulous frosty decorations using toothpicks, plastic-foam spheres, white spray paint, and spray-on snow. Begin by poking flat-sided toothpicks into plastic-foam spheres, placing the picks as close together as possible, and cover the entire sphere. Spray-paint the whole sculpture white; cover it with spray-on snow and let dry. Group the sculptures on the mantel or a tabletop. If you use candles with them, make sure the flames aren't close to the wooden picks and extinguish the flames when you leave the room.

Transform a window or doorway opening into a simple tree by suspending small ball ornaments from a ribbon-wrapped tension rod, *right*. Use narrow ribbon to hang the top ball and fishing line for the others. Add a wired-ribbon bow as a tree topper.

You'll be surprised how easy it is to turn plain ball ornaments into delightful dazzlers, *below left* and *right*. It doesn't take much more than a little bit of ribbon, spray paint, and glue to give ordinary ornaments swinging new style. Ornament instructions begin on *page 56*.

1 Velvet two-tone ribbon adds a touch of luxury to a plain pink ornament. Simply hot-glue six lengths of ribbon around the sides of the ball and glue ribbon loops on top so they drape over the ball. For the topper, fold over ribbon three times, going back and forth, so it looks as if you laid three bows on top of each other. Make a final loop around the center of the layered ribbon, and tie or glue it to the ball.

2 If you have old ball ornaments whose paint has seen better days, embellish the peeling or faded surface with beads or ball chain in a swirling pattern for a mottled look that sparkles on a lighted tree. To remove even more paint before embellishing the ornament, apply hot-glue to the ball in swirling shapes; let dry. Carefully peel off the dried glue; hot-glue the beads or ball chain to the ornament in a swirled pattern that doesn't match the peeled paint.

3 Transform an uninteresting clear-ball ornament into a showcase for a recipient's name or a holiday greeting. Remove the metal top and add a small amount of paint to the inside of the ball through the opening, swirling it around until it sticks and starts to dry. Let the paint dry; put the top back on. Use stencils and acrylic paint to personalize the ball with a name or a short holiday greeting (on the outside). Tie a pink bow to the top.

4 Reach into the scrap pile to turn short lengths of green ribbon into an ornament with flapper style. Cut 5/8-inch ribbon into 1½- and 2-inch-long strips (for an average-size ornament). Glue the strips to the ball, starting at the bottom with three rows of shorter strips and finishing the middle and top with longer strips.

5 No sequins or baubles on hand? Grab split peas from your kitchen cabinet and glue them to a red ornament to create a fun and festive polka-dot pattern.

Jazz up a plain glass-ball ornament in a jiff by embellishing it with favorite Christmas phrases. Use a fine-tip silver paint pen to write "Merry Christmas" or other holiday-inspired words or phrases, such as "Noel," "Peace on Earth," or "Ho, Ho, Ho" in concentric circles around the ball. Vary the colors of the paint pens and the ornaments to suit your decor. If you're not a wordsmith, use the paint pens to draw simple holiday shapes, such as trees, snowmen, or snowflakes on the ornaments—or distribute ornaments and paint pens to family members to encourage self-expression.

1

2

3

4

5

6

6 Turn an out-of-style ornament into a bauble with personality. Cover an unsightly hue with a light coating of light-green acrylic paint; let dry. Add a second coat and rub off some paint while it's wet. To ruffle a striped wire-edge ribbon, pull one side of the wire. Hot-glue the pulled side to the top of the ornament, letting the rest fluff out.

7 Seed beads add instant glamour to a once homely plastic ornament. Coat the ornament with matte-silver spray paint; let dry. Glue on beads to create glistening vertical stripes and finish with a big silver bow.

8 You've seen clear plastic ornaments in craft stores—but what to do with them? Give them a snowball-like appearance with artificial snow filling and add snowflake stickers to the sides; top each one with a bead-chain bow.

7

8

In a Twinkling Instructions

Tiny Trees

Curled Leaf Tree

shown on page 40

MATERIALS
6-inch-diameter basket container
Florist's foam
Hot-glue gun and glue sticks
16-inch length of ¼-inch-diameter wooden dowel
Brown acrylic paint and paintbrush
12-inch-tall plastic-foam cone
Green sheet moss
Small twigs
Fine wire
Fresh bay leaves
Purchased eight-point silver-star pick
Artificial floral berries (filler for top of basket)

INSTRUCTIONS
Cut a block of florist's foam to fit the bottom of the basket; hot-glue in place. Paint the dowel brown; let dry.

Press the dowel into the center bottom of the plastic-foam cone and into the center of the florist's foam in the basket. Adjust the depth of the dowel until a trunk space of 4 inches remains between the basket and the cone. Glue the dowel in place; let dry.

Cover the exposed florist's foam in the basket with green sheet moss; hot-glue in place. Arrange twigs around the dowel trunk, wrapping wire around the twigs to secure in place.

Working from bottom to top, attach rows of bay leaves placed side by side. Glue the stem end of the leaves to the cone, overlapping rows about one half the length of the leaves. The tips of the bay leaves curl as they dry in 2–3 days' time.

Insert the stick end of the star into the top of the cone. Cover the moss-covered florist's foam with artificial floral berries.

Tinkertoy Tree

shown on page 40

MATERIALS
One large container of Tinkertoys
Foil
Small pot, crock, or mug
Small ornaments

INSTRUCTIONS
Place eight equal-size rods in a wheel. Assemble rows of branches in graduating sizes; put the tree together by placing a center rod between the horizontal layers of the branches. Build the tree from bottom to top, starting with larger rods and working to the top small rods. Place the tree in a small pot, crock, or mug. Add a foil star at the top and slide a few small baubles onto the branches.

Beaded Topiaries

shown on page 38

MATERIALS
12-, 16-, and 20-inch plastic-foam cones
Plastic-bead garlands in two different bead diameters
Crafts glue
Moss-color acrylic paint
Pearl aerosol paint
Glaze
Foam brush
Micro fine silver glitter

INSTRUCTIONS
Wrap and glue the plastic-bead garlands around the cone, alternating the sizes to create a stripe effect until the entire cone is covered. Let the adhesive dry. Line a shadow box with newspaper and place the cone in the box. Spray a base coat of pearl paint, which will make covering the bead surface with acrylic paint easier. Mix two parts acrylic paint with one part water. Paint the cone, taking care to press the brush between the beads to apply some paint to the plastic-foam base; let dry. If needed, apply another coat of the paint mixture for solid coverage. Once the paint has dried, apply the glaze to the tree with a brush. Immediately sprinkle a heavy coat of glitter onto the wet glaze. Let dry thoroughly.

Towering Pines

shown on page 39

MATERIALS

Tracing paper
White illustration board
Scissors: sharp-tip and scallop-edge
Crafts knife and metal straightedge
1/16-inch circle punch
Acrylic crafts paints: light green, medium green, and dark green
Sponge brush
Spray adhesive
Super-fine glitter: black, green, and white
Clear-drying glue in a fine-tip dispenser
Glass glitter

INSTRUCTIONS

Trace the tree patterns at *right* onto tracing paper for the small tree. Enlarge the patterns at 125 percent for the medium tree and 150 percent for the large tree using a photocopier. Cut out the shapes.

Trace each of the tree-star shapes once on illustration board and each of the tree shapes twice; there are three pieces for each size of tree. Cut out the pieces with sharp-tip scissors. Make the center slits in each piece with a crafts knife and metal straightedge. Use the crafts knife to cut away the interior areas of the branches. Trim the bottom edge of each branch with scallop-edge scissors and make 1/8-inch holes along the bottom edge of each branch with the hole punch.

Paint the pieces for the small tree light green, the medium tree dark green, and the large tree medium green. Let the paint dry.

Spray one side of the three large tree pieces with adhesive and immediately sprinkle with green glitter. Turn the pieces over and repeat to apply glitter to the remaining sides. In this same manner, apply a mixture of green and white glitter to both sides of the small tree pieces and a mixture of green and black glitter to both sides of the medium tree pieces.

Use the fine-tip glue dispenser to apply glue to the star and to outline the open areas on one side of each tree piece. Immediately sprinkle glass glitter on the wet glue. When the glue is dry, repeat on the opposite sides of the tree pieces.

Assemble the trees, sliding the same-size pieces together. Evenly spread the pieces apart to stand the trees upright.

TOWERING PINES
Small Tree Pattern
Cut 1 tree with star
Cut 2 trees without stars

Slit

BEESWAX CANDLE BOW
Bow Pattern

BEESWAX CANDLE BOW
Knot Pattern

BEESWAX CANDLE BOW
Tail Pattern
Cut 2

Centerpieces
Beeswax Candle Bow
shown on page 44

MATERIALS
Tracing paper
Red honeycomb beeswax sheets
Crafts knife
Red candle glitter
Hair dryer
5×6-inch red pillar

INSTRUCTIONS
Trace the patterns at *right* onto tracing paper; cut out the shapes. Lay the pattern pieces on beeswax and use a crafts knife to cut around the shapes, cutting one bow, one bow knot, and two bow tails. Refer to the photo, *above,* for what the cut pieces look like (the bow has already been shaped in the photo; the long strip wraps around the purchased candle).

Lay the bow piece flat and bring each end in to overlap at the center. Press in place and cover the bow with glitter. Wrap the bow knot around the center of the bow, molding the knot into shape. Slightly overlap and press together the narrow ends of the bow tails. Cover them with glitter. Press the parts of the bow together, using a hair dryer to warm the wax to make it slightly tacky. Coat the bow with glitter.

Cut a 1⅜-inch-wide strip of beeswax long enough to reach around the pillar. Press the bow on the center of the strip. Cover the band with glitter. Wrap the strip around the candle, using the hair dryer to attach the strip firmly to the candle if necessary.

Other Great Ideas
Sweater Throws & Pillows
shown on page 51

MATERIALS
Old wool sweaters
Liquid dishwashing soap
Matching sewing threads
Steam stabilizer
Felted wool fabric (optional)
Pinking shears
Pillow form
Yarn and large-eye needle (optional)

INSTRUCTIONS
Felt the Sweaters
Gather sweaters that are at least 80 percent wool. (See Felting Tips, *page 62,* for general guidelines.) The number of sweaters needed will depend on the desired size of the finished piece and the size of the sweaters after shrinkage. We used approximately 12 sweaters for a throw and two sweaters for a pillow. Use sweaters with patterns or designs for interest, such as the reindeer rectangles for the throw and the skier rectangle for the pillow.

Sort the sweaters by color. Place sorted sweaters, turned inside out, into the washing machine set to hot wash/cold rinse; add a small amount of liquid dishwashing soap. Add a few lint-free items such as old T-shirts or jeans; they provide friction as the machine agitates to promote the felting. If desired, remove the sweaters two or three times during the wash cycle and rinse in cold water, squeezing out excess fluid; extreme temperature changes help to speed the felting process.

Remove sweaters before the entire spin cycle is complete and roll in a towel to remove excess water. Shape and allow to air-dry. Repeat the felting process until stitches are no longer visible. The felted sweaters should be dense and thick. If the knitting stitches show more than you like, repeat the process. If necessary, hand-felt for additional firmness and smoothness by rubbing the item on a washboard with hot water and liquid dishwashing soap or rolling it between palms. Let dry; trim excess fuzziness with scissors.

Remove the sleeves from the sweaters and cut along the inner arm seams to lay flat. Cut the body of the sweater along the side and shoulder seams. Lay the felted pieces on a flat surface to cut the shapes needed.

Assemble the Throw or Pillow
Throw: Our patchwork throw measures 48×60 inches. Cut twenty-eight 8¼×10¼-inch rectangles from a variety of solid-color felted sweater pieces. From patterned felted sweater pieces, cut four 8¼×10¼-inch rectangles and one 17×21-inch rectangle.

Lay the rectangles on a flat surface, positioning the patterned rectangles as shown in the Assembly Diagram on *page 62.* When satisfied with the arrangement, assemble the small rectangles into eight four-patch units, referring to the diagram. To create a four-patch unit, first sew two small rectangles together in pairs.

Sew the four-patch units together in rows in the same manner, inserting the large patterned rectangle into the center of the middle row. To complete the throw, sew the three rows together.

Pillows: Measure to find the dimensions of the desired pillow form; add 1 inch to each for seam allowances. Use these measurements to cut a pillow front and back from the felted sweater pieces. With wrong sides facing and a ½-inch seam allowance, sew the pillow front to the back, leaving the bottom edge open. Turn the pillow cover right side out. Insert the pillow form through the bottom opening. Slip-stitch the opening closed.

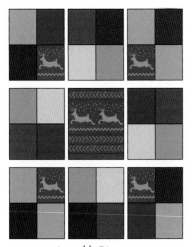

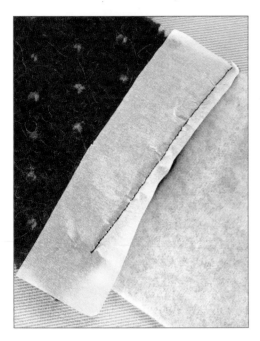

Assembly Diagram

For a pieced pillow front, such as the skier pillow, cut squares and rectangles from felted pieces, allowing for seam allowances. Sew the pieces together with right sides facing. Press the seam allowances open. Sew the pillow front to back and turn right side out. Use yarn to embroider along the edges of the design if desired. Insert the pillow form and slip-stitch the opening closed.

Felting Tips

Felting is a process that involves washing wool items in hot water to tightly bond the stitches so the fabric can be cut without instantly unraveling. The process shrinks the item and can dramatically change its appearance. That's where the fun comes in.

Felting is a fickle process; you never quite know what you'll end up with. Let these tips and considerations guide you in your recycled-sweater felting projects:

Take a test run. If you're new to felting, select a sweater that's not crucial to your design. Wash it and observe how the fabric transforms itself. Note how it changes in appearance, thickness, and size with each successive washing.

Successful felting occurs when the stitches visually disappear. However, there are times when it's best not to let the felting go too far (especially if you're felting items where fit matters, such as mittens). Remove the felted item from the washer when you think it has reached the size you want. You can always put it back in for another wash if you want it smaller. If you remove it in the middle of a wash cycle, hand-rinse it in cold water and roll in a towel to remove excess water.

Try to use pure-wool sweaters. Though you can work with wool/acrylic blends, 100 percent wool sweaters give more consistent results. Thrift stores and garage sales are good places to find old sweaters. Remember that you can cut around holes or stains; just make sure the garment will provide enough good fabric. If you really catch the felting craze, you can buy sweaters by the pound online.

Washing promotes felting. The felting process can shrink an item from about 15 to 20 percent across its width and from 25 to 40 percent in length. Machine-drying should be avoided since it only shrinks, not felts, an item.

Tread lightly. Sweaters may require multiple washings to get the desired results. Check the garment frequently and stop the process when you have the look you want.

Bundled-Up Snow Family

shown on page 53

MATERIALS

Unfinished wooden snowmen: two 6½-inch and one each
  8- and 10-inch (available from *www.dottiemcgrathstudios.com*)
Sandpaper: 100- and 150-grit
Tack cloth
Latex primer
Paintbrushes: 1-inch flat, small round, and stencil
Gloss acrylic paints: white and black
Stencil paint creme: blue (we used Delta Stencil Magic Paint
  Creme: Cottage Blue)
Blue acrylic paint
Wool felt: purple, green, red, and blue
Sewing needle and matching sewing thread
Fabric paint: light green, purple, and white
Pinking shears and scallop-edge scissors
Buttons: three each of ¾-inch blue and red, three ½-inch
  purple, two ½-inch green, and one ¾-inch snowflake
Mandarin Orange Fimo Soft Polymer Clay
T-pin
Metal baking sheet
Aluminum foil
Hot-glue gun and glue sticks
Polyester fiberfill (optional)

INSTRUCTIONS

Sand all surfaces of the snowmen with 100- and then 150-grit sandpaper. Remove the sanding dust with a tack cloth. Apply primer; let the primer dry. Lightly sand again and wipe clean. Paint all surfaces of the snowmen gloss white. When the paint is dry, use a stencil brush and Cottage Blue to lightly shade the edges of each snowman; let dry. Thin blue acrylic paint with water and use it to add stitch lines ¼ inch from the edges of the snowmen.

For the purple snowman, cut a 1½×14-inch scarf strip and an 8½×4-inch hat rectangle from purple felt. Cut 1-inch slits for fringed scarf ends. Overlap the 4-inch edges of the hat to fit the head; sew the overlap together. Cut 1-inch slits along the top edge of the hat to fringe; tie thread around the hat just below the fringe. Fold up 1 inch at the bottom edge for a cuff. Use purple fabric paint to add dots to the scarf ends and cuff; let dry.

For the green snowman, use pinking shears to cut a 1½×14-inch scarf strip and an 8½×4-inch hat rectangle from green felt. Overlap the 4-inch edges of the hat to fit the head; sew overlap together. Tie thread around the hat 1 inch from the top. For the cuff, fold up 1 inch on the bottom edge. Use light green fabric paint to add stripes to the scarf ends and cuff; let dry.

For the red snowman, cut a 2×18-inch scarf strip, one 7-inch hat circle, and one 3½×10-inch hat brim from red felt. Trim the short ends of the scarf with scallop-edge scissors. Make running stitches close to the edge of the hat circle; pull the thread ends to fit it on the snowman's head. Knot the thread and evenly distribute the gathers. Sew the gathered edge to one long edge of the brim, overlapping the brim at the back; sew the overlap together. Fold the brim twice to measure 1¾ inches wide. Paint white zigzag lines on the scarf ends and hat brim; let dry.

For the blue snowman, cut a 2¼×19-inch scarf strip and an 11×7-inch hat rectangle from blue felt. To fringe, cut 1¼-inch slits at each end of the scarf. Overlap the 7-inch edges of the hat to fit the snowman's head; sew the overlap together. Cut 1-inch slits along the top edge of the hat to fringe; tie thread around the hat just below the fringe. Fold up 1 inch twice at the bottom edge for a cuff. Glue a snowflake button to the hat center front.

Knead the clay until it is smooth and pliable. Form it into a cone-shape nose for each snowman, about 1 to 1½ inches long and ⅜ to ½ inch wide at the base. Twist the nose slightly, swirling the clay to resemble a carrot. Press the base against a flat surface. Press a T-pin into the clay to make grooves, going around the nose. Follow the manufacturer's instructions to bake the noses on an aluminum-foil-covered baking sheet. Let the noses cool.

Refer to the photographs to finish each snowman. Attach the nose and buttons with hot glue. Dip the end of a paintbrush into black gloss paint and dot the eyes; let dry. Place the hat on the head and secure with hot glue, stuffing with a small amount of fiberfill, if desired. Tie the scarf around the neck and tack in place with hot glue.

Whether they're near or far, send someone special your good tidings with a festive card or thoughtful gift.

Giving

Send a holiday greeting with a Christmas-tree card decorated with tiny ornaments. Fold a piece of crimson card stock in half, and add a cutout tree and a tied ribbon to the cover. Tiny ornaments complete the joyful holiday greeting. Instructions are on *page 85.*

It's in the Mail

Think you don't have time for custom-made cards? Now you do. Simple cutouts, minimal embellishments, and clean designs make these cards quick to create assembly-line-style.

Traditional Christmas wishes benefit from a retro card with bright, festive colors, *above*. Make the frame by cutting and piecing prestitched ribbon and then suspend a charm from a string to take the place of the "o" in Noel. Instructions are on *page 85*.

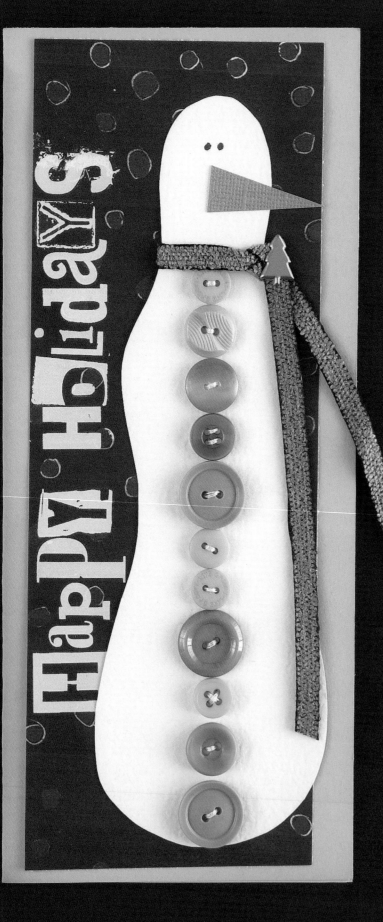

This frosty fellow, *left,* may look time-consuming to make with his plethora of buttons, but prestitching the buttons with a bit of thread and then gluing them to his front will speed up the process. Spell out the greeting with rub-on letters in mixed fonts for an eclectic look. Instructions and a pattern are on *page 84.*

Unleash your inner artist by using acrylic paint to rub the circles over heat-embossed snowflakes on the card, *above.* Machine-stitch red circles around each motif, but don't worry about being perfect—irregular lines add to the charm of the card. Instructions are on *page 84.*

Need a card on a smaller scale? This berry gift tag uses purchased embellishments on a hand-cut tag base. Instructions are on *page 85*.

to: Ciara

Decorating the tree has a second go-around with this tree-shaped gift-card holder. A loop attached to the top of the tree wraps over the star button to secure the front cover. When unlooped, the tree pulls downward to reveal the pocket that shows the gift card. Instructions begin on *page 86*.

Under Wraps

Make your gift wrap as enticing as the surprise inside.
Wrap your presents—both big and small—using these
creative packaging ideas.

What's on everyone's wish list these days? Gift cards! They may seem like an impersonal cop-out to creative types, but you can up the giving appeal by skipping the store's packaging options for a homemade felt holder. This ribbon-wrapped rhinestone-studded holder, *above*, is pretty as a package. It's also multifunctional: Use it to announce the menu of a holiday dinner or to hold a party favor.

Gift cards stowed in plain paper envelopes can easily get lost in a flurry of packages under the tree. No worries here! Rickrack transforms this festive red-and-white card holder, *left*, into a pocketbook-like tree ornament. Hang it on a bough so it—and its contents—stay clear of the floor-level frenzy on Christmas eve.

Instructions begin on *page 86*.

Dress a plain white box in perfect party attire by gluing on playful red buttons, *above.* Border the buttons with holiday-hue striped ribbons and finish with a green pinstriped bow. Instructions are on *page 86.*

Papers with candy-cane stripes and red polka dots on white, *right,* fit the season. Finish a package with a purchased holly-trimmed frame setting off a festive "ho, ho, ho" greeting. Instructions are on *page 85.*

These red-and-white gift tags are eye-candy inspiration for turning a mundane gift into a special gesture—no fancy paper required! Gussy up a plain white package with handmade tags embellished with rubber stamps, or try these other fun, fast ideas.

• Add tiny embellishments, such as pom-poms at the center and tips of the snowflake tag, top right.

• Create three-dimensional flourishes with simple cutouts, such as the harlequin-stamped tree, second row right, or purchased accents, such as the poinsettia, second row center.

• A beaded twist of crafts wire, such as on the star tag, top left, also makes a fun embellishment. Even a small ornament can dangle on a box.

• For an adornment, bottom right, cut a circle in a piece of patterned paper, poke a small hole in the paper above the circle, and tie on an ornament with thin twine. Use photo corners to attach the "frame" to the box.

have yourself a merry little christmas

merry christmas

merry christmas

Merry Christmas

Tartan-plaid fabric, a ribbon bow, and greenery turn a plain paint can—purchased empty at a home improvement store—into a cookie container with traditional charm.

Turn a plain paint can into a wintry vision in silver with the addition of metallic paper and a band of bejeweled ribbon. Instructions are on *page 86.*

Dress up plain-Jane cups
by gluing a kicky band of scrapbooking border just below the rim. Set the sugar-cube-filled mug on a rectangular plate and add a tea ball and lidded clear tubes packed with loose-leaf teas. Identify the contents with computer-generated labels and add bright bows for a festive finish.

Give a gardener a gift with growth potential. Make flowerpots and saucers look great with coats of glossy white paint, *left*. Use a foam brush to paint the pot and saucer rims red; add dots to the pot with the end of an artist's brush and red crafts paint. Fill the container with potting soil and packets of herb seeds. Flip the saucer atop the pot and tie them together with a ribbon. Tuck a trowel and a rosemary sprig in the bow to remind your botany-minded buddy that spring is just around the corner.

Treat a coffee-consuming pal to an oversize cuppa joe, *right*. Temporarily trim a large latte bowl with glued-in-place red rickrack; fill the vessel with chocolate-covered espresso beans or freshly roasted coffee beans. Give the bistro-inspired still life a café-au-lait twist by nestling a white napkin folded to resemble a whopping dollop of whipped cream in the center of the beans. To re-create this frothy fabric center, see the napkin-folding diagram on *page 87.*

The *Bow* Guide

Making florist-perfect bows is easy. Just follow our step-by-step instructions to fashion beautiful embellishments for packages, wreaths, and much more.

Pom-Pom Bow

1   2   3   4   5

Step 1 Form a ribbon circle that's approximately the width of your bow. Ours measures about 6 inches. Continue winding ribbon around for the number of loops you want. We wound our ribbon 8 times.

Step 2 Flatten the loops, and using scissors, make a diagonal cut at each corner.

Step 3 Refold the flattened loops, matching the notches in the center. Firmly tie a thin piece of ribbon or wire around the center.

Step 4 Working on one side of the bow, pull out the innermost loop and twist it to the right. Pull out the next innermost loop and twist it to the left. Continue in this way until all loops on one side have been twisted. Repeat for the other side of the bow.

Step 5 Arrange the loops as needed to make the bow. Use the thin ribbon or wire ends to attach the bow to your project.

Chrysanthemum Bow

1   2   3   4   5

Step 1 Form a ribbon circle that's approximately the width of your bow. Ours measures about 5 inches. Continue winding ribbon around for the number of loops you want. We wound our ribbon 9 times.

Step 2 Flatten the loops, and using scissors, make a diagonal cut at each corner.

Step 3 Refold the flattened loops, matching the notches in the center. Firmly tie a thin piece of ribbon or wire around the center.

Step 4 Make evenly spaced, narrow cuts into the loops. Pull out the loops as described in Step 4 for the Pom-Pom Bow, *above.*

Step 5 Arrange the loops as needed to make your bow. Use the thin ribbon or wire ends to attach the bow to your project. *Note: Use only nonfraying ribbon for this bow.*

Poinsettia Bow

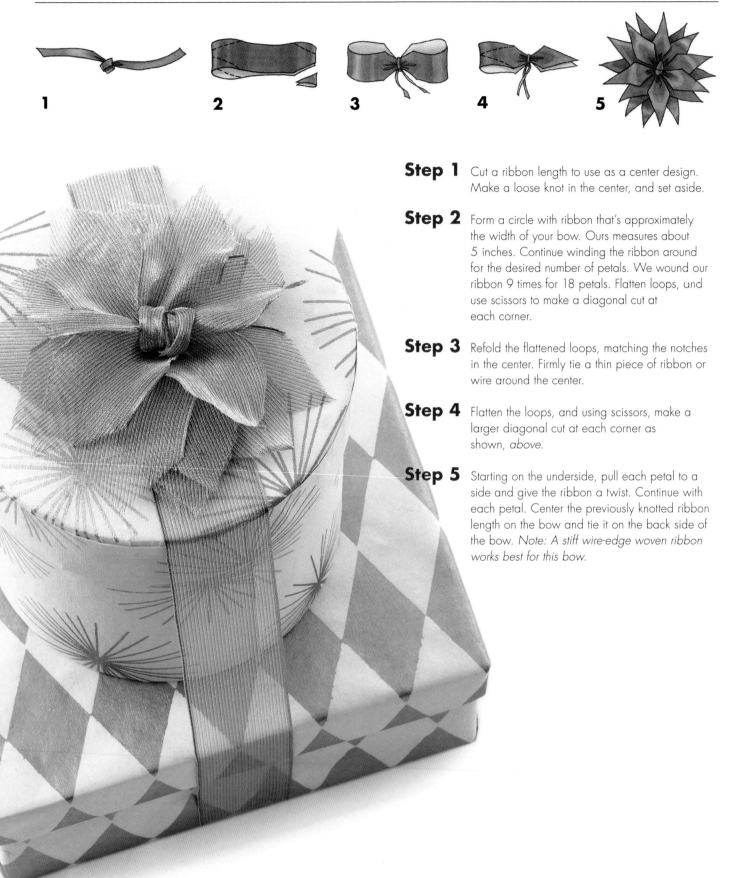

1 **2** **3** **4** **5**

Step 1 Cut a ribbon length to use as a center design. Make a loose knot in the center, and set aside.

Step 2 Form a circle with ribbon that's approximately the width of your bow. Ours measures about 5 inches. Continue winding the ribbon around for the desired number of petals. We wound our ribbon 9 times for 18 petals. Flatten loops, and use scissors to make a diagonal cut at each corner.

Step 3 Refold the flattened loops, matching the notches in the center. Firmly tie a thin piece of ribbon or wire around the center.

Step 4 Flatten the loops, and using scissors, make a larger diagonal cut at each corner as shown, *above*.

Step 5 Starting on the underside, pull each petal to a side and give the ribbon a twist. Continue with each petal. Center the previously knotted ribbon length on the bow and tie it on the back side of the bow. *Note: A stiff wire-edge woven ribbon works best for this bow.*

Florist's Bow

 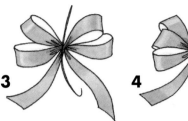 

1 **2** **3** **4** **5**

Step 1 Determine the tail length for your bow and twist the ribbon at this point, keeping the right side of the ribbon facing you.

Step 2 Make a loop and give the ribbon a twist. Holding the twist between your thumb and index finger, make a second loop the same size in the opposite direction. Give this loop a twist.

Step 3 Continue making same-size loops in this way until the bow has the fullness you want. Insert wire through the bow center, twisting the tails together at the back of the bow.

Step 4 Finish by forming a small loop for the bow center. Cut the ribbon, leaving a matching tail length. Insert wire through the bow center, twisting the tails together at the back of the bow. Trim the wire, leaving long tails.

Step 5 Arrange the loops as needed to make your bow. Use the wire tails to attach the bow to your project.

Dior Bow

1 **2** **3** **4**

Step 1 Cut four pieces of ribbon in graduating lengths. Form the pieces into loops and secure with glue.

Step 2 Flatten and secure the loops in the center with glue.

Step 3 Cut another piece of ribbon and wrap it around the center.

Step 4 Secure the wrapped ribbon on the back side of the bow with glue. *Note: We layered two ribbons for additional interest on our bow.*

Giving Instructions

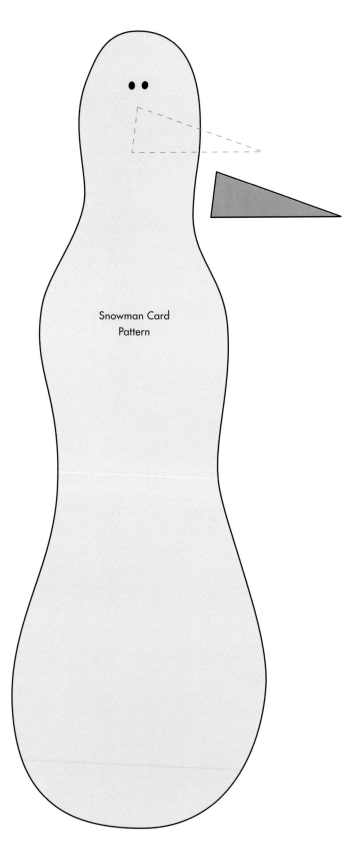

It's in the Mail

Happy Holidays Snowman Card
shown on page 68

MATERIALS
Card stock: blue, white, orange
Red patterned paper
Various rub-on letters
Narrow blue ribbon
Silver button (we used a tree)

INSTRUCTIONS
Fold a sheet of blue card stock and fold in half. Cut a 4½×9½-inch rectangle from red patterned paper. Glue the red patterned paper rectangle to the blue card stock rectangle.

Using a variety of rub-on letters in different fonts, spell out a holiday greeting along the left edge of the red patterned paper, leaving enough space for the snowman to be positioned to the right of the letters.

Use the pattern at *right* to cut the snowman from white card stock and the nose from orange card stock. Glue the pieces to the red patterned paper. Add details such as an orange card stock triangle for a nose, hand-drawn eyes, a ribbon scarf, and buttons.

Snowman Card Pattern

Happy Holidays Snowflake Card
shown on page 68

MATERIALS
Card stock: white
Snowflake rubber stamp
Clear embossing ink
Clear embossing powder
Heat-embossing tool
Blue acrylic paint
Red thread and sewing machine
Red rubber-stamp ink

INSTRUCTIONS
Cut a 4×4-inch square from white card stock and fold it in half. Stamp snowflakes on the front of the card using clear embossing ink. While the ink is still wet, sprinkle clear embossing powder onto the stamped snowflakes. Use the heat-embossing tool to heat the stamped images until the powder melts and turns clear and shiny.

Rub blue acrylic paint in a circle over each heat-embossed snowflake; let dry. Stitch red circles around each snowflake. Don't worry about stitching perfect circles; rough circles add to the playful look of the card. Stamp the greeting on a scrap of white card stock. If desired, ink the edges of the scrap and the card base with red rubber-stamp ink.

Joy to the World Card
shown on page 66

MATERIALS
Red card stock
Green card stock
Glue stick or double-stick tape
Self-adhesive mini pop-dots
Ornament stickers
Narrow satin ribbon
Rub-on phrase

INSTRUCTIONS
Cut a piece of red card stock 7½ inches square and fold it in half. Referring to the photo for the shape, cut out a tree from the green card stock. Adhere the tree to the front of the card. Press dots to the back of each ornament. Press in place on the tree. Wrap ribbon around the front flap of the card. Tie in a bow. Use a rub-on phrase to add a greeting.

Berry Gift Tag
shown on page 69

MATERIALS
Checked scrapbooking paper
Glue stick or double-stick tape
2×4-inch precut rectangular shipping tag
Filigree holly-and-berries trim

INSTRUCTIONS
Cut a 1½×3-inch piece of scrapbooking paper. Use a glue stick or double-stick tape to adhere the paper to the center of the tag. Peel the self-adhesive backing from the holly embellishment and press onto the corner of the tag.

Noel Ornament Card
shown on page 67

MATERIALS
Striped scrapbooking paper
Off-white card stock
Prestitched grosgrain ribbon
Crafts glue
Double-stick tape
Embroidery floss
Ornament charm

INSTRUCTIONS
Cut scrapbooking paper to 6×10 inches; fold in half widthwise. Cut card stock to measure 3½×5 inches. Cut ribbon into four equal lengths. Cut each end at an angle to create a 3½×5-inch frame. Type the letters "n," "e," and "l" on a computer, allowing enough space for the charm to represent the "o" in "noel." Glue

the ribbon to the card-stock rectangle to make a frame. Press the frame in place in the center of the folded striped card using tape. Tie embroidery floss to the charm and finish with a bow. Glue the ornament in place on the front of the card to complete the word.

Under Wraps
Striped Gift Box
shown on page 72

MATERIALS
Tall square box with lid
Striped and polka-dot scrapbooking papers
Wide green ribbon
Hot-glue gun and glue sticks
Mini frame
Holly-berry trim

INSTRUCTIONS
Wrap base of box in striped paper and lid of box in polka-dot paper. Wrap ribbon around box vertically; hot-glue in place. Wrap a piece of ribbon around a loop of ribbon to make a bow, and glue it to the lid. Hot-glue holly-berry trim to the corner of the frame, and glue the frame to the gift.

Buttons-and-Bows Wrap

shown on page 72

MATERIALS

White mailer box
Hot-glue gun and glue sticks
¾-inch red buttons
Medium-width ribbons

INSTRUCTIONS

Evenly space and hot-glue the red buttons down the center of the box. Cut two lengths of ribbon; wrap a length around the box on either side of the buttons, and hot-glue in place. Tie a simple bow around the box.

Paper-Covered Paint Can

shown on pages 74 and 75

MATERIALS

New, unused metal paint can
Three sheets of 12×12-inch scrapbook paper (same color or print)
Crafts knife
Spray adhesive
Ribbon

INSTRUCTIONS

Trim each sheet of scrapbook paper to 11×11 inches (two for the can body, one for the lid). Lightly mist the back side of each sheet with spray adhesive just before applying it to the can.

Align one sheet of paper along the upper edge of the back of the can, just under the upper lip, and smooth the sheet onto the can (see diagram, *top right*). Use the bottom lip of the can as a guide to score the paper with your thumbnail or the smooth bottom of a crafts knife. Cut away the excess paper along the scored edge using a very sharp crafts knife (a sharp blade makes clean edges).

To fit the paper around the handles, smooth the paper by pushing your thumb up to the handle; use a crafts knife to slice through from that point to the edge of the paper (see Diagram, *top right*). Continue pushing the paper close to the handle and trimming away the excess as you go to make a neat opening. (Less-than-perfect openings can be covered with cording.) Cover the front of the can in similar fashion.

For the lid, trim a sheet of paper slightly larger than the can lid and mist the back with spray adhesive. Attach the sheet to the lid and score around the inner rim, carefully cutting away any excess paper.

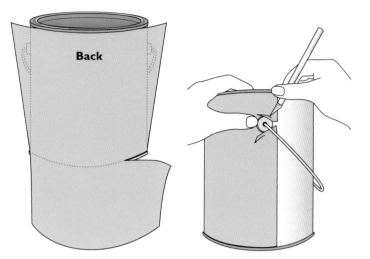

Paper-Covered Paint Can Diagrams

Gift-Card Holders

shown on pages 70 and 71

MATERIALS

FOR EACH HOLDER
Scallop-edge scissors or pinking shears
Matching sewing threads

RHINESTONE-STUDDED HOLDER
4×6½-inch rectangle of white felt
⅝ yard of ⅝-inch-wide red striped ribbon
Decorative rhinestones
Fabric glue

TREE-SHAPE HOLDER
Tracing paper
Felt: white and green
Nine ⅜-inch-diameter red buttons
1-inch-diameter gold star button
2½-inch length of gold elastic cording

RICKRACK HANGING HOLDER
Felt: 4×7¾-inch rectangle of white and
    two 1½×7¾-inch strips of red
6-inch length of red mini rickrack
¾-inch-diameter red button

INSTRUCTIONS

Rhinestone-Studded Holder: Center an 8-inch length of ribbon lengthwise on the white felt rectangle; turn under the ends. Attach ribbon to the felt by sewing down the center of the ribbon.

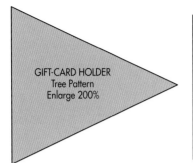

GIFT-CARD HOLDER
Tree Pattern
Enlarge 200%

GIFT-CARD HOLDER
Tree-shape Pattern
Enlarge at 200%

Fold up 2 inches at the bottom of the felt to form a pocket with the ribbon on the outside. Sew 1/8 inch from the side edges of the pocket. Fold down 1¾ inches at the top for the front flap; press lightly. Trim the sides of the gift-card holder with the scallop-edge scissors.

Glue rhinestones onto the front of the holder. Tie a bow with the remaining ribbon and tack to the center top on the front of the holder.

Tree-Shape Holder: Trace the patterns, *above,* onto tracing paper; cut out the shapes. Use the patterns to cut one holder from white felt and one tree from green felt, cutting the tree with pinking shears. Fold the rectangular area of the white felt in half to form the pocket. Sew 1/8 inch from the side edges of the pocket.

Position the tree on the triangular area of the white felt on the outside of the holder and sew in place 3/16 inch from the edges of the tree. Hand-sew the red buttons on the tree. Fold the tree flap up to close the holder; press lightly. Mark the placement for the star and sew a star button to the front of the pocket. Fold the elastic cord in half and tack the ends to the back of the tree flap, adjusting the length as needed to fit over the star.

Rickrack Hanging Holder: Trim the long edges of each felt piece with pinking shears. Position the red strips on the white rectangle slightly in from the side edges. To form the handle, tuck ½ inch at each end of the rickrack under an inside edge of the red strips 2 inches from the top edge of the felt pieces. Sew the red strips in place close to the long edges, catching the rickrack ends in the stitching.

Fold up 2¾ inches at the bottom of the felt to form a pocket with the red strips on the outside. Sew the side edges of the pocket atop the outer stitching line of each red strip. Fold down 2 inches at the top for the front flap; press lightly. To shape the front flap, trim from the center bottom to a point ¾ inch below the top corners.

Cut a vertical slit in the center section of the flap large enough to accommodate the button. Sew the button to the pocket under the slit.

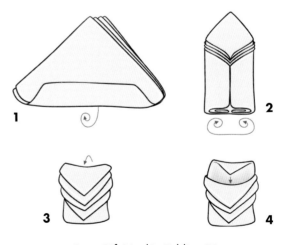

Latte Gift Napkin-Folding Diagram

The tree is trimmed,
the gifts are wrapped,
and the greetings have
been sent—now get
ready for a festive
gathering with friends
and family.

Entertaining

AppetizersDrinks

It's the biggest party season of the year, so mix and mingle
while enjoying this sampling of tasty hors d'oeuvres and
festive, conversation-sparking sippers.

Light and flaky phyllo dough topped with a Swiss cheese and tomato filling make these miniature Tomato Quiche Tartlets, *opposite*, a treat you'll want to enjoy even when Christmas is over.

Warm your guests' palettes with this soothing, citrus-spiced Cranberry-Raspberry Sipper, *left.* Mull it in a slow-cooker to keep it at the ready while the buffet line forms and guests socialize.

Recipes are on page 104.

Go nuts with these satisfying spirals, *right,* filled with a feta and pine nut spread. Refrigerated pizza dough speeds up the prep time. To turn the filling into a nutty dip, skip the pizza dough and stir in a little milk. Recipe is on *page 104.*

The secret to these crispy cilantro crab cakes, *left,* is a generous coating of panko, or Japanese-style bread crumbs. Serve the warm cakes with a dollop of zesty aïoli made with serrano peppers. Recipe is on *page 105.*

Give the phrase "Nutcracker Suite" a whole new meaning with this plate full of tempting, nutty appetizers, *opposite.* Clockwise from top left: Macadamia-Pear Bruschetta, Pesto-Hazelnut Cheese Pâté, and Nutty Layered Cheese Spread. Recipes begin on *page 105.*

Tap into the coffee craze to update classic chocolate fondue, *opposite.* The results will please coffee and chocolate lovers alike—not only do the coffee crystals and liqueur add a hint of java taste, but they help intensify the chocolate flavor, too. Recipe is on *page 106.*

Top each frothy serving of this tropical Coconut Eggnog, *above,* with a soft and dreamy pillow of sweetened whipped cream. Recipe is on *page 106.*

After dinner, your guests will clamor for this frothy Spiced Orange Mocha, *right.* Top each serving with a spoonful of Whipped Honey-Orange Topping. Recipe is on *page 107.*

Carry on the age-old tradition of garnishing a cake roll to make it resemble a log. Shape marzipan into leaves and berries or use fresh mint leaves and raspberries. Recipe is on *page 108*.

Sweets & Treats

Whether you exchange your holiday treats with friends and family or just bake up a batch to enjoy at home, you'll enjoy this collection of cookies and desserts.

Don't be fooled by the sedate, homey look of these crackled cookies, *left*. They're packed with ground almonds and flavored with coffee liqueur, making them perfect for any party or occasion. Recipe is on *page 109*.

With these elegant treats, *above*, you can offer your guests the best of everything—a tender chocolate cookie, buttery caramel, chewy pecans, and satiny drizzles of chocolate. Recipe is on page *107*.

It doesn't get any easier than Crème de Menthe Brownies, *above*—mixed in one pan and topped with a simple minty frosting. Recipe is on *page 108.*

As perfect as a mound of sparkling white snowballs, these mouthwatering Toffee-Almond Sandies, *opposite,* make a great gift wrapped up in a fabric-covered box. Recipe begins on *page 109.*

Looking for a spectacular dessert to top off your holiday dinner? Decadent Chocolate-Almond Mousse Cake, *left,* is the perfect choice. Recipe is on *page 109.*

Luscious peaks of meringue curl around frozen ice cream and cake to make Frosty Baked Alaskas. Sprinkle a light shower of snowy powdered sugar onto the plates just before serving. Recipe is on *page 110*.

Delicate and crisp, these feathery snowflakes melt on your tongue just like the real thing. Recipe is on *page 110.*

Dried fruits make this traditional Greek baklava even more tempting than usual. Recipe begins on *page 110*.

Lovers of coffee and chocolate will clamor to sample these distinctive dipped sticks. A cookie press makes shaping the ripply sticks easy. Recipe is on *page 111*.

Start with versatile Mocha Magic Dough to make the tasty base for these delicious Coconut-Pecan Mocha Triangles. Recipes are on *page 111*.

Entertaining Recipes

Appetizers & Drinks

Tomato Quiche Tartlets

Prep: 15 minutes **Bake:** 10 minutes **Oven:** 325°F
shown on page 90

- 2 2.1-ounce packages baked miniature phyllo dough shells (30 shells)
- ½ cup finely snipped dried tomato (not oil-packed)
- 2 eggs, slightly beaten
- 3 tablespoons half-and-half, light cream, or milk
- 1½ teaspoons snipped fresh basil or ½ teaspoon dried basil, crushed
- Dash salt
- Dash ground black pepper
- ¾ cup finely shredded Swiss cheese (3 ounces)

1. Preheat oven to 325°F. Place phyllo dough shells on a baking sheet; set aside.

2. For filling, in a small bowl, combine dried tomato and enough boiling water to cover; let stand for 2 minutes. Drain well. In a medium bowl, combine eggs, half-and-half, basil, salt, and pepper. Stir in soaked dried tomato and Swiss cheese.

3. Spoon about 2 teaspoons of the filling into each phyllo shell. Bake for 10 to 15 minutes or until filling is slightly puffed and a small knife inserted into the centers of the tartlets comes out clean. Serve warm or cool. *Makes 30 tartlets.*

MAKE-AHEAD TIP: Prepare and bake tartlets as directed; cool. Place tartlets in an airtight container and chill for up to 24 hours. Place tartlets on a baking sheet. Bake in a 300°F oven about 10 minutes or until heated through.

Cranberry-Raspberry Sipper

shown on page 91
Prep: 15 minutes **Cook:** 5 to 6 hours (low) or 2½ to 3 hours (high)

- 1 small orange
- 8 cups cranberry-raspberry drink
- ¼ cup packed brown sugar
- 6 inches stick cinnamon
- 3 star anise
- 1 teaspoon whole cloves
- Thin orange peel strips (optional)
- Star anise (optional)

1. Use a vegetable peeler to remove the orange portion of the orange peel. Cut peel into strips. Squeeze juice from orange; discard seeds and pulp. In a 3½-, 4-, or 5-quart slow cooker, combine orange juice, cranberry-raspberry drink, and brown sugar.

2. For spice bag, cut a double thickness of 100 percent cotton cheesecloth into an 8-inch square. Place the peel strips from the orange, cinnamon, 3 star anise, and cloves in center of the cheesecloth square. Bring corners of cheesecloth together; tie with 100 percent cotton string. Add to slow cooker.

3. Cover and cook on low-heat setting for 5 to 6 hours or on high-heat setting for 2½ to 3 hours.

4. To serve, remove spice bag and discard. Ladle drink mixture into 10 heatproof cups. If desired, garnish with thin orange peel strips and star anise. *Makes 10 servings.*

Feta and Pine Nut Spirals

Prep: 25 minutes **Bake:** 18 minutes
shown on page 92

- 1 3-ounce package cream cheese, softened
- ½ cup crumbled feta cheese with garlic and herb (2 ounces)
- 3 tablespoons pine nuts or finely chopped almonds, toasted
- 3 tablespoons finely chopped pitted ripe olives
- 2 tablespoons snipped fresh parsley
- 1 tablespoon milk
- 1 10-ounce package refrigerated pizza dough (for 1 crust)
- Olive oil
- Ground black pepper

1. Preheat oven to 375°F. Grease a baking sheet; set aside.

2. For filling, in a small bowl, stir together cream cheese, feta cheese, nuts, olives, parsley, and milk. Set aside.

3. On a lightly floured surface, roll pizza dough into a 14×10-inch rectangle. Cut dough in half crosswise to form two 10×7-inch rectangles. Spread half of the filling onto each dough rectangle to within 1 inch of edges. Starting from a long side, roll up each rectangle into a spiral. Seal seam and ends. Place spirals, seam sides down, on prepared baking sheet. Brush surface of spirals with oil; sprinkle with pepper.

4. Bake for 18 to 20 minutes or until golden. Cool on baking sheet on a wire rack for 5 minutes. Using a serrated knife, cut spirals into 1-inch-thick slices. Serve warm. *Makes 20 spirals.*

Cilantro Crab Cakes
with Serrano Aïoli

Prep: 25 minutes   **Cook:** 6 minutes per batch

shown on page 92

2   eggs
1   medium red sweet pepper, finely chopped
½   of an 8-ounce can water chestnuts, drained and finely chopped (½ cup)
½   cup panko (Japanese-style bread crumbs) or fine dry bread crumbs
2   tablespoons snipped fresh cilantro
½   teaspoon salt
¼   teaspoon ground white pepper or ground black pepper
1   16-ounce can crabmeat, drained, flaked, and cartilage removed
⅔   cup panko (Japanese-style bread crumbs) or fine dry bread crumbs
¼   cup cooking oil
1   recipe Serrano Aïoli (below)
    Fresh cilantro sprigs (optional)
    Lime wedges (optional)

1. In a large bowl, use a fork to beat eggs slightly. Stir in sweet pepper, water chestnuts, the ½ cup bread crumbs, snipped cilantro, salt, and white pepper. Add crabmeat; mix well. Form mixture into about thirty 1½-inch-wide patties.

2. Place the ⅔ cup bread crumbs in a shallow dish; dip patties into bread crumbs, turning to coat. In a large skillet, heat 2 tablespoons of the oil over medium heat. Add half of the crab cakes; cook for 6 to 8 minutes or until golden, turning once. Drain on paper towels; keep warm. Repeat with remaining 2 tablespoons oil and remaining crab cakes.

3. Serve crab cakes warm with Serrano Aïoli. If desired, garnish with cilantro sprigs; serve with lime wedges. *Makes about 30 crab cakes (15 servings).*

Serrano Aïoli: In a small bowl, combine ⅔ cup mayonnaise or salad dressing; 1 tablespoon lime juice; 1 to 2 fresh serrano peppers, seeded and finely chopped*; ½ teaspoon salt; and ¼ teaspoon ground white pepper or ground black pepper. Cover and chill for up to 24 hours. Makes ¾ cup.

Make-Ahead Directions: Prepare and form crab cakes as directed through Step 1. Cover and chill for up to 24 hours. To serve, continue as directed in steps 2 and 3.

*Test Kitchen Tip: Because chili peppers contain volatile oils that can burn your skin and eyes, avoid direct contact with them as much as possible. When working with chili peppers, wear plastic or rubber gloves. If your bare hands do touch the peppers, wash your hands and nails well with soap and warm water.

Pesto-Hazelnut Cheese Pâté

Prep: 25 minutes   **Chill:** 8 to 24 hours

shown on page 93

8   ounces goat cheese (chèvre)
2   3-ounce packages cream cheese, softened
1   cup fresh basil leaves
½   cup fresh spinach leaves
¼   cup grated Parmesan cheese
2   tablespoons fresh flat-leaf parsley
2   tablespoons pine nuts
1   clove garlic, quartered
3   tablespoons olive oil
¼   cup finely chopped hazelnuts (filberts) or pecans, toasted

1. Line two 4½×2½×1½-inch loaf pans with plastic wrap, leaving enough excess to cover.

2. In a food processor, combine goat cheese and cream cheese. Cover and process until smooth; set aside.

3. For basil-spinach pesto, in the clean food processor, combine the 1 cup basil, the spinach, Parmesan cheese, parsley, pine nuts, and garlic. Cover and process until a paste forms. With machine running, gradually add olive oil, processing until almost smooth.

4. Onto the bottom of each of the prepared pans, spread about ⅓ cup of the goat-cheese mixture. Top each with 1 tablespoon hazelnuts, half of the basil-spinach pesto, another 1 tablespoon hazelnuts, and another ⅓ cup of the cream cheese mixture.

5. Cover with plastic wrap and chill for 8 to 24 hours.

6. To serve, invert loaf onto a platter; remove and discard plastic wrap. If desired, slice and serve pâté on toasted French bread slices; garnish with coarsely chopped hazelnuts and basil leaves. *Makes 16 servings.*

Nutty Layered Cheese Spread

Stand: 30 minutes   **Prep:** 30 + 20 minutes   **Chill:** 2 to 24 hours

shown on page 93

3   cups finely shredded Swiss cheese (12 ounces)
½   of an 8-ounce package cream cheese
⅓   cup dairy sour cream
1   tablespoon horseradish mustard or Dijon-style mustard
1   cup chopped pistachio nuts, walnuts, and/or pecans, toasted

1. In a large bowl, combine Swiss cheese and cream cheese; let stand at room temperature for 30 minutes.

2. Add sour cream and mustard. Beat with an electric mixer on medium speed until mixture is slightly fluffy.

3. Line a 7½×3½×2-inch loaf pan with plastic wrap, leaving enough excess to cover. Set aside ¼ cup of the nuts. Sprinkle one-fourth of the remaining nuts evenly into pan. Spoon one-fourth of the cheese mixture onto nuts; spread gently to flatten. Repeat layering cheese and nuts, one-fourth at a time, pressing into pan to make even layers. Sprinkle with 2 tablespoons of the reserved nuts, pressing to adhere.

4. Cover with plastic wrap and chill for 2 to 24 hours.

5. To serve, invert loaf onto a platter; remove and discard plastic wrap. Let stand for 20 minutes before serving. Press remaining 2 tablespoons reserved nuts onto sides. If desired, slice and serve on melba toast, baguette slices, party rye, and/or crackers. *Makes 20 servings.*

Macadamia-Pear Bruschetta

Start to finish: 25 minutes
shown on page 93

8 ounces sweet bread (such as Portuguese sweet bread, brioche, or Hawaiian sweet bread)
2 tablespoons butter or margarine, melted
1 pear, peeled and sliced
1 tablespoon packed brown sugar
1 tablespoon lime juice
½ teaspoon ground cinnamon
¼ teaspoon ground allspice
3 ounces Brie cheese, cut into 24 pieces
⅓ cup coarsely chopped macadamia nuts or almonds

1. Preheat oven to 350°F. Cut bread into ½-inch-thick slices. Trim crusts from bread slices. Brush both sides of each slice with melted butter. Cut bread into 2-inch squares. Place on a baking sheet. Bake about 10 minutes or until lightly toasted, turning once.

2. Meanwhile, in a small bowl, combine sliced pear, brown sugar, lime juice, cinnamon, and allspice.

3. Preheat broiler. Top each bread square with a piece of cheese, some pear mixture, and a few nuts; press gently to secure nuts. Broil 4 to 5 inches from heat for 2 to 3 minutes or until cheese begins to melt and nuts are lightly toasted. Serve warm. *Makes 24 servings.*

Mocha Fondue

shown on page 94

4 ounces sweet baking chocolate, broken up
4 ounces semisweet chocolate, chopped
⅔ cup half-and-half, light cream, or milk
½ cup sifted powdered sugar
2 teaspoons instant coffee crystals
2 tablespoons coffee liqueur (optional)
 Assorted fruits, such as star fruit slices, pineapple chunks, kiwi fruit wedges, strawberries, pear slices, and banana slices
 Orange-peel slivers (optional)

1. Combine chocolates, cream, sugar, and coffee crystals in a heavy medium saucepan. Stir over low heat until chocolates are melted and smooth. Remove from heat; stir in the coffee liqueur, if desired. Pour into a fondue pot; keep warm over low heat. Serve with fruit as dippers. If desired, garnish with orange peel. *Makes 12 servings.*

Coconut Eggnog

shown on page 95

3 cups milk
6 eggs yolks, beaten
1 15- to 16-ounce can cream of coconut
½ cup light rum
2 teaspoons vanilla
½ cup whipping cream
1 tablespoon sugar

1. In a medium saucepan, stir together milk and egg yolks. Cook and stir just until mixture comes to boil; remove from heat. Immediately stir in cream of coconut, rum, and vanilla. Transfer to a pitcher or punch bowl. Cover and chill in the refrigerator about 3 hours or until cold.

2. To serve, in a chilled medium mixing bowl, beat cream and sugar with chilled beaters of an electric mixer on medium speed until soft peaks form (tips curl). Serve over eggnog. *Makes ten 4-ounce servings.*

Spiced Orange Mocha

Start to finish: 15 minutes
shown on page 95

½ cup packed brown sugar
4 ounces semisweet chocolate, cut up
2 ounces unsweetened chocolate, cut up
1 tablespoon finely shredded orange peel
½ teaspoon ground cinnamon
4 cups hot brewed coffee
1 cup half-and-half or light cream, warmed
1 recipe Whipped Honey-Orange Topping (see recipe, below)
   Finely shredded orange peel (optional)

1. In a blender container, combine brown sugar, semisweet chocolate, unsweetened chocolate, the 1 tablespoon orange peel, and the cinnamon. Cover and blend until chocolate is finely chopped. Remove half of the chocolate mixture; set aside. Add 2 cups of the hot coffee to the blender container; cover and blend at medium speed until chocolate is melted. Add ½ cup of the half-and-half or light cream; cover and blend until frothy. Pour into 4 coffee mugs or cups.

2. In the blender container, combine reserved chocolate mixture and remaining coffee. Cover and blend at medium speed until chocolate is melted. Add remaining half-and-half or light cream; cover and blend until frothy. Pour into 4 more coffee mugs or cups. Top each serving with a spoonful of Whipped Honey-Orange Topping and, if desired, additional shredded orange peel. *Makes 8 servings.*

Whipped Honey-Orange Topping: In a chilled medium mixing bowl, combine ½ cup *whipping cream*, 1 tablespoon *honey*, and, if desired, 1 tablespoon *orange liqueur or orange juice*. Beat with chilled beaters of an electric mixer on medium speed until soft peaks form (tips curl).

Sweets & Treats

Chocolate-Caramel Thumbprints

Prep: 30 minutes   **Chill:** 2 hours   **Bake:** 10 minutes per batch
Oven: 350°F
shown on page 97

1 egg
½ cup butter, softened
⅔ cup sugar
2 tablespoons milk
1 teaspoon vanilla
1 cup all-purpose flour
⅓ cup unsweetened cocoa powder
¼ teaspoon salt
16 vanilla caramels, unwrapped
3 tablespoons whipping cream
1¼ cups finely chopped pecans
½ cup semisweet chocolate pieces
1 teaspoon shortening

1. Separate egg. Cover and chill egg white until needed. Set egg yolk aside.

2. In a large bowl, beat butter with an electric mixer on medium to high speed for 30 seconds. Add sugar and beat well. Beat in the egg yolk, milk, and vanilla.

3. In a medium bowl, stir together the flour, cocoa powder, and salt. Add flour mixture to butter mixture; beat until well mixed. Wrap cookie dough in plastic wrap; chill about 2 hours or until easy to handle.

4. Preheat oven to 350°F. Lightly grease cookie sheets; set aside. In a small saucepan, combine caramels and whipping cream; heat and stir over low heat until mixture is smooth. Set aside.

5. Beat the egg white with a fork. Place egg white in a shallow dish. Place pecans in another shallow dish. Shape dough into 1-inch balls. Roll balls in egg white; roll in nuts to coat. Place balls 1 inch apart on prepared cookie sheets. Using your thumb, make an indentation in the center of each ball.

6. Bake about 10 minutes or until edges are firm. Spoon some of the melted caramel mixture into indentation of each cookie. (If necessary, reheat caramel mixture to keep it spoonable.) Transfer cookies to wire racks and cool.

7. In another small saucepan, combine chocolate pieces and shortening; heat and stir over low heat until melted and smooth. Let cool slightly. Drizzle cookies with chocolate mixture. Let stand until chocolate is set. *Makes 36.*

Chocolate-Raspberry Yule Log

Prep: 30 minutes **Stand:** 30 minutes **Bake:** 12 minutes
Oven: 375°F **Freeze:** 6 hours + 2 hours to 1 week
shown on page 96

4   eggs
⅓   cup all-purpose flour
¼   cup unsweetened cocoa powder
1   teaspoon baking powder
¼   teaspoon salt
½   teaspoon vanilla
⅓   cup granulated sugar
½   cup granulated sugar
    Sifted powdered sugar
1   teaspoon raspberry liqueur (optional)
¾   cup seedless raspberry preserves
1   quart French vanilla ice cream
    Rich Chocolate Frosting
    Purchased marzipan (optional)
    Red decorative sugar (optional)

1. Separate eggs. Allow egg whites and egg yolks to stand at room temperature for 30 minutes.

2. Preheat oven to 375°F. Grease a 15×10×1-inch jelly-roll pan; line with waxed paper. Grease and flour the waxed paper; set pan aside. In a small bowl, stir together flour, cocoa powder, baking powder, and salt; set aside.

3. In a medium bowl, combine egg yolks and vanilla. Beat with an electric mixer on high speed about 5 minutes or until thick and lemon-colored. Gradually add the ⅓ cup granulated sugar, beating on high speed until sugar is almost dissolved.

4. Thoroughly wash the beaters. In a large bowl, beat egg whites with an electric mixer on medium speed until soft peaks form (tips curl). Gradually add the ½ cup granulated sugar, beating until stiff peaks form (tips stand straight). Fold egg yolk mixture into beaten egg whites. Sprinkle flour mixture over egg mixture; fold in gently just until combined. Spread batter evenly in the prepared pan.

5. Bake for 12 to 15 minutes or until cake springs back when lightly touched. Immediately loosen edges of cake from pan and turn cake out onto a towel sprinkled with powdered sugar. Remove the waxed paper. Roll up towel and cake into a spiral, starting from one of the cake's short sides. Cool on a wire rack.

6. Unroll cake and remove towel. If desired, stir raspberry liqueur into raspberry preserves. In a chilled large bowl, stir ice cream with a wooden spoon just until softened enough to spread. Spread ice cream on cake to within 1 inch of the edges. Spread raspberry preserves on ice cream to within 1 inch of edges. Roll up cake; wrap in foil. Freeze for 6 hours.

7. Spread Rich Chocolate Frosting over cake roll. Using the tines of a fork, score the frosting lengthwise so it resembles tree bark. Cover and freeze for at least 2 hours or up to 1 week.

8. Let stand at room temperature for 10 minutes before serving. If desired, shape marzipan into holly leaves and holly berries; roll berries in red decorative sugar. Garnish log with marzipan berries and leaves. *Makes 10 servings.*

Rich Chocolate Frosting: In a heavy, small saucepan, combine 3 ounces *unsweetened chocolate* and 3 tablespoons *butter*. Heat and stir over low heat until chocolate melts. Remove from heat. Add 1½ cups sifted *powdered sugar* and ¼ cup *milk*, stirring until smooth. Add 1½ cups sifted powdered sugar; stir in enough additional milk (1 to 2 tablespoons) to make of spreading consistency. Spread immediately over cake roll.

Crème de Menthe Brownies

shown on page 98

½   cup butter
2   ounces unsweetened chocolate, cut up
1   cup granulated sugar
2   eggs
¼   teaspoon mint extract
⅔   cup all-purpose flour
¼   cup butter
1½ cups sifted powdered sugar
2   tablespoons green crème de menthe
1   ounce semisweet chocolate
    Layered chocolate-mint candies, chopped (optional)

1. Preheat oven to 375°F. Grease a 9×9×2-inch baking pan; set aside.

2. In a heavy medium saucepan, melt ½ cup butter and unsweetened chocolate over low heat. Remove from heat. Stir in granulated sugar, eggs, and mint extract. Beat lightly by hand until just combined. Stir in flour.

3. Spread batter in prepared pan. Bake in the preheated oven for 20 minutes. Cool completely in pan on a wire rack.

4. In a medium mixing bowl, beat ¼ cup butter with an electric mixer on low to medium speed until fluffy. Gradually add 1 cup of the powdered sugar. Beat in crème de menthe. Gradually beat in remaining powdered sugar to make of spreading consistency.

5. Spread crème de menthe mixture over brownies. Melt semisweet chocolate in a small heavy saucepan over low heat. Drizzle chocolate over brownies. Sprinkle with chopped candies, if desired. Cut into triangles or bars. *Makes 16 to 20 bars.*

Mocha-Almond Cookies

Prep: 45 minutes **Chill:** 1 hour **Bake:** 13 minutes per batch
Oven: 325°F
shown on page 97

½   cup unsalted butter
4   ounces unsweetened chocolate, cut up
6   tablespoons coffee liqueur
¾   cup granulated sugar
4   eggs
1⅓ cups all-purpose flour
¾   teaspoon baking powder
1   cup blanched almonds, finely ground
    Sifted powdered sugar

1. In a small saucepan, combine butter and chocolate; heat and stir over low heat until melted. Remove from heat; stir in coffee liqueur. Set aside.

2. In a large bowl, combine granulated sugar and eggs. Beat with an electric mixer on medium speed until combined. Stir chocolate mixture into egg mixture. In a small bowl, stir together flour and baking powder; add to the chocolate-egg mixture, stirring until combined. Stir in almonds. Cover dough and chill about 1 hour or until firm.

3. Preheat oven to 325°F. Divide dough in half; refrigerate one portion. Form remaining portion into 1-inch balls. Roll balls in powdered sugar, coating well. Place balls 2 inches apart on an ungreased cookie sheet. Bake about 13 minutes or until firm. Transfer cookies to wire racks and cool. Repeat with remaining dough. *Makes 60 cookies.*

Chocolate-Almond Mousse Cake

Prep: 45 minutes **Stand:** 2 hours **Bake:** 350°F **Chill:** 2 to 4 hours
shown on page 98

6   eggs
2   teaspoons vanilla
1¼   cups sugar
1   cup all-purpose flour
¼   cup unsalted butter, melted
3   ounces bittersweet chocolate, chopped, melted, and cooled
2   tablespoons amaretto
     Chocolate Mousse Frosting
     Bittersweet and/or milk chocolate curls
¼   cup sliced almonds, lightly toasted

1. Let eggs stand at room temperature for 30 minutes. Grease one 9×5×3-inch loaf pan and one 9×9×2-inch baking pan. Line the bottom of each pan with parchment paper. Grease the paper and lightly flour each pan; set aside. Preheat oven to 350°F.

2. Combine eggs and vanilla. Beat with an electric mixer on high speed until frothy. Gradually add 1 cup sugar, beating 7 to 10 minutes or until light yellow. Sift ⅓ cup flour over egg mixture;

gently fold in. Repeat twice. Fold in butter. Spread 1½ cups of batter in the loaf pan. Fold melted chocolate into remaining batter; spread chocolate batter into 9×9×2-inch pan.

3. Bake the 9×5×3-inch loaf pan about 15 minutes and 9×9×2-inch baking pan about 20 minutes or until the tops spring back. Cool in pans on wire racks 10 minutes. Remove from pans; peel off paper. Cool on racks. Cut chocolate cake in half, making two 9×4½-inch layers. Trim cakes to the same length.

4. For syrup: In a small saucepan, bring ¼ cup water and remaining ¼ cup sugar to boiling, stirring to dissolve sugar. Remove from heat. Stir in amaretto. Cool to room temperature.

5. Brush one chocolate layer with about one-third of the syrup. Spread with ⅔ cup frosting. Top with vanilla cake; brush with another one-third of the syrup. Spread with another ⅔ cup frosting. Top with remaining chocolate cake layer; brush with remaining syrup. Spread remaining frosting over top and sides of cake layers. Cover and refrigerate for at least 2 hours or up to 4 hours.

6. To serve, let stand at room temperature 30 minutes. Pile chocolate curls and almonds on top. *Serves 16 to 20.*

Chocolate Mousse Frosting: Place 5 ounces finely chopped *bittersweet chocolate* in a bowl. Bring ½ cup *whipping cream* to boiling; pour over chocolate. Let stand 3 minutes. Gently whisk until smooth. Let stand 1 hour, whisking occasionally. About 10 minutes before chocolate mixture is finished cooling, in a 1-cup glass measuring cup, mix 2 tablespoons *cold water* and ½ teaspoon *unflavored gelatin*. Let stand 2 minutes. Place cup in a saucepan of boiling water (water should come about halfway up the sides of the cup). Cook and stir about 1 minute or until gelatin is completely dissolved. Remove cup from saucepan. Stir in 1 tablespoon *amaretto*. Gradually drizzle gelatin mixture over 1½ cups *whipping cream* while beating on medium speed. Beat just until stiff peaks form (tips stand straight). Stir 1 cup of the whipped cream mixture into the chocolate mixture. Fold the chocolate mixture into remaining whipped cream mixture.

Toffee-Almond Sandies

Prep: 25 minutes **Bake:** 15 minutes per batch **Cool:** 1 hour
Oven: 325°F
shown on page 99

1   cup butter
½   cup packed brown sugar
1   tablespoon water
1½   teaspoons vanilla
2¼   cups all-purpose flour
1   cup finely chopped sliced almonds
1   cup sifted powdered sugar

1. Preheat oven to 325°F. In a large mixing bowl, beat butter with an electric mixer on medium speed for 30 seconds. Add brown sugar. Beat until combined, scraping side of bowl. Beat in the water and vanilla. Beat in as much of the flour as you can with the mixer. Stir in any remaining flour. Stir in almonds.

2. Shape dough into 1-inch balls. Place balls 1 inch apart on ungreased cookie sheets. Bake for 15 minutes or until bottoms are light brown. Transfer cookies to wire racks; cool completely. If desired, store in an airtight container in the freezer for up to 1 month.

3. Spoon powdered sugar into a plastic bag. Add cooled or thawed cookies; shake to coat. Arrange in decorative containers for gift giving. *Makes about 48 cookies or four 1 dozen cookie gifts.*

Frosty Baked Alaskas

Prep: 25 minutes **Freeze:** 2 to 24 hours **Bake:** 3 minutes
Oven: 450°F
shown on page 100

6   slices loaf sponge cake or pound cake cut ½ to ¾ inch thick
3   to 6 teaspoons desired flavor liqueur or orange juice*
6   scoops desired flavor ice cream*
¾   cup water
1½ cups sifted powdered sugar
¼   cup meringue powder
    Sifted powdered sugar (optional)

1. If desired, use a 3-inch round cookie cutter to cut cake slices into rounds. On an ungreased baking sheet, arrange cake slices. Sprinkle with liqueur or orange juice. Place a scoop of ice cream on each. Cover and freeze for at least 2 hours or up to 24 hours.

2. Preheat oven to 450°F. For meringue, in a large mixing bowl, stir together ½ cup of the powdered sugar and the meringue powder. Stir in the water. Beat with an electric mixer on high speed for 5 minutes. Gradually beat in the remaining 1 cup powdered sugar.

3. Spread the meringue onto each cake and ice cream stack. Bake for 3 minutes or until top of meringue is golden.

4. If desired, sprinkle 6 dessert plates with additional powdered sugar. Place meringue-covered stacks on dessert plates; serve immediately. *Makes 6 servings.*
    Note: *Think about matching liqueurs and ice creams, such as amaretto with chocolate-almond ice cream, coffee liqueur with mocha ice cream, Chambord with strawberry ice cream, or crème de menthe with chocolate-mint ice cream.*

Meringue Snowflakes

Prep: 1 hour **Bake/dry:** 1 hour **Oven:** 300°F
shown on page 101

2   egg whites
¼   teaspoon cream of tartar
1⅓ cups sifted powdered sugar
    Desired food coloring (optional)
    Plain or colored coarse sugar or decorating candies

1. Let egg whites stand at room temperature for 30 minutes. Line 3 cookie sheets with parchment paper; set aside.

2. Preheat oven to 300°F. In a medium mixing bowl, beat egg whites and cream of tartar with an electric mixer on high speed until soft peaks form (tips curl). Add powdered sugar, 1 tablespoon at a time, beating well after each addition. If desired, add food coloring. Beat mixture for 7 minutes on high speed. (Mixture should be thick and glossy but may not be stiff.)

3. Spoon mixture into a decorating bag fitted with a medium star tip (1/16-inch opening). Making lines about ¼ inch thick, pipe 4- to 5-inch snowflake shapes about 2 inches apart onto prepared cookie sheets. Sprinkle with coarse sugar or candies.

4. Place cookie sheets in oven. Turn off oven. Let meringues dry in the oven with the door closed about 1 hour or until dry and crisp but still white. Cool on cookie sheets on wire racks.

5. Carefully cut parchment paper around snowflakes. Using your hands, gently peel parchment away from snowflakes. Store in an air-tight container in a cool, dry place for up to 1 week. *Makes 10 to 12 cookies.*

Fruit-and-Nut Baklava

Prep: 35 minutes **Bake:** 45 minutes **Oven:** 325°F
shown on page 102

1   cup butter, melted
32 sheets frozen phyllo dough (14x9-inch rectangles), thawed
3   cups Greek Fruit-and-Nut Filling (recipe opposite)
1¼ cups sugar
½   cup water
1   teaspoon finely shredded lemon peel or orange peel
¼   cup lemon juice or orange juice
3   tablespoons honey
    Sugared Rosemary and Cranberries (optional)

1. Preheat oven to 325°F. Brush the bottom of a 13×9×2-inch baking pan with some of the melted butter. Unfold phyllo dough. Layer eight sheets of phyllo in prepared baking pan, brushing each sheet with melted butter. (While you work, keep the remaining phyllo covered with plastic wrap to prevent it from drying out.) Sprinkle 1 cup of the Greek Fruit-and-Nut Filling on top of the phyllo layers in pan. Repeat layering phyllo and filling two more times. Layer remaining phyllo sheets over filling in the pan, brushing each sheet with butter. Drizzle any remaining butter over the top.

2. Using a sharp knife, cut through all layers to make diamond-shape pieces, replacing any dough that pulls up while cutting.

3. Bake for 45 to 50 minutes or until golden. Transfer to wire rack.

4. *For syrup:* In medium saucepan, stir together sugar, the water, lemon or orange peel, lemon or orange juice, and honey. Bring mixture to boiling; reduce heat. Simmer, uncovered, for 20 minutes.

5. Pour hot syrup over baklava in pan. Cool completely. Use a knife to separate pieces. If desired, garnish baklava with Sugared Rosemary and Cranberries. *Makes about 32 pieces.*

Sugared Rosemary and Cranberries: Lightly brush fresh rosemary sprigs and fresh cranberries with light-colored corn syrup. Sprinkle with sanding sugar or granulated sugar.

Greek Fruit-and-Nut Filling

3½ cups walnuts, finely chopped (about 14 ounces)
1   cup dried cranberries, finely chopped
¾   cup dried apples, finely chopped
¾   cup golden raisins, finely chopped
⅓   cup sugar
2   teaspoons ground cinnamon

1. In a large bowl, stir together walnuts, dried cranberries, dried apples, raisins, sugar, and cinnamon. Use for Fruit-and-Nut Baklava. *Makes 5 cups.*

Mocha Magic Dough

2   cups butter, softened
1⅓ cups sugar
⅓   cup unsweetened cocoa powder
2   teaspoons instant espresso powder or instant coffee powder
1½ teaspoons baking powder
2   eggs
1½ teaspoons vanilla
4   cups all-purpose flour

1. In a large bowl, beat butter with an electric mixer on medium to high speed for 30 seconds. Add sugar, cocoa powder, espresso powder or coffee powder, baking powder, and ½ teaspoon salt; beat until combined. Beat in eggs and vanilla. Beat in as much of the flour as you can with the mixer. Using a wooden spoon, stir in the remaining flour.

2. Divide dough in half. Use for Chocolate-Dipped Mocha Sticks and Coconut-Pecan Mocha Triangles. (While making first recipe, let remaining dough stand at room temperature until needed or up to 1 hour.) *Makes 2 portions.*

Chocolate-Dipped Mocha Sticks

Prep: 20 minutes   **Bake:** 10 minutes per batch   **Oven:** 375°F
shown on page 103

1   portion Mocha Magic Dough (recipe at left)
1½ cups semisweet chocolate pieces
1   tablespoon shortening
    White nonpareils (optional)

1. Preheat oven to 375°F. Pack unchilled Mocha Magic Dough portion into a cookie press fitted with a ½-inch star plate. Force dough through press onto ungreased cookie sheet in stick shapes 4 inches long, placing them 1 inch apart. Bake 10 to 12 minutes or until edges are firm. Cool on sheet 1 minute. Transfer to a wire rack; cool.

2. In a small, heavy saucepan, combine chocolate and shortening; heat and stir over low heat until melted and smooth. Dip an end of each cookie into chocolate mixture. If desired, sprinkle chocolate with white nonpareils. Place on waxed paper; let stand until chocolate is set. *Makes about 24 sticks.*

Coconut-Pecan Mocha Triangles

Prep: 10 minutes   **Bake:** 20 minutes   **Oven:** 375°F
shown on page 103

1   portion Mocha Magic Dough (recipe at left)
1   egg, slightly beaten
1   5-ounce can (⅔ cup) evaporated milk
⅔   cup sugar
¼   cup butter
1   teaspoon instant espresso powder or instant coffee powder
1¼ cups chopped pecans
1   cup flaked coconut

1. Preheat oven to 375°F. Line 13×9×2-inch baking pan with heavy-duty foil. For crust: Press Mocha Magic Dough portion into prepared pan. Bake 20 minutes or until edges are lightly browned and begin to pull away from sides of pan. Remove from oven; cool.

2. For topping: In heavy, medium saucepan, combine egg, evaporated milk, sugar, butter, and espresso or coffee powder. Cook and stir over medium heat for 6 to 8 minutes or until bubbly and thickened. Remove from heat; stir in pecans and coconut. Cover and cool for 15 minutes. Spread cooled topping over crust. Lift cookie from pan using foil. Cut into 2-inch squares; cut each square diagonally to form triangles. Cover and store in refrigerator. *Makes 48 triangles.*

Better Homes and Gardens®
Creative Collection®

Editorial Director John Riha

Editor in Chief Deborah Gore Ohrn

Executive Editor Karman Wittry Hotchkiss

Managing Editor Kathleen Armentrout

Contributing Editorial Manager Heidi Palkovic

Contributing Design Director Tracy DeVenney

Copy Chief Mary Heaton
Contributing Copy Editor Dave Kirchner
Proofreader Joleen Ross
Administrative Assistant Lori Eggers

Publishing Group President
Jack Griffin

President and CEO Stephen M. Lacy

Chairman of the Board William T. Kerr

In Memoriam
E. T. Meredith III (1933–2003)

CONTRIBUTORS

Designers
Rita Anderson: pages 55 (top) and 73.
Artful Offerings: page 17 (ornaments 6 and 7).
Faith Berven: page 7.
Cathy Blackstone: page 70.
Tari Colby: page 17 (ornament #9).
Laura Collins: page 17 (ornament #5).
Jackie Dickie: pages 55 (top) and 73.
Phyllis Griffiths: page 12.
Mary Heaton: page 17 (ornament #2).
Lori Hellander: page 48 (top left).
Heather Hill: pages 39, 44 (top), 53, 59, 70, 71, 76, and 77.
Jennifer Keltner: page 17 (ornament #3).
Elaine Koonce: pages 44 (bottom left and right) and 49 (top right).
Brenda Lesch: page 17 (ornament #4).
Karen Lidbeck-Brent: page 7, 8 (left and right), and 13.
Matthew Mead: page 52.
Carrie Naumann: page 56.
Plaid Enterprises: page 17 (ornaments #1 and #8).
Carol Schalla: page 14.
Alison Ventling: pages 7, 10, and 38.
Wanda Ventling: pages 7, 10, 38, 18, 19, 20, 21 (left), 41, 51 (right and left), 55 (bottom left and bottom right), 57 (all), and 58 (all).
Deb Wiley: page 7.

Illustrators
Glenda Aldrich: pages 29, 30, 31, 33, 35, 84, and 87 (bottom).
Chris Neubauer: pages 32, 59, 62 (top), and 87 (top).
Ann Weiss: pages 79, 80, and 83.

Photographers
Craig Anderson: page 24 (top left).
King Au: pages 27, 54, 73, 74, and 75.
Marty Baldwin: page 57 (all).
Graham Brown: pages 47 (bottom), 49 (bottom), and 98 (bottom).
Kim Cornelison: pages 6, 7, 10, 14, 16, 17 (ornaments #8 and #9), 26 (top left), 38, 43, 46, 47 (top), 48, and 49 (top left).
Mike Dieter: pages 92 (top), 93, and 97 (left).
Colleen Duffley: cover and page 9.
John Reed Forsman: page 55 (top).
Bill Geddes: page 52 (left).
Tria Giovan: pages 24 (top right) and 24 (bottom).
Bill Hopkins: pages 21 (right), 25, 40 (right), 41, 42, 44 (bottom right), and 50.
Jon Jensen: pages 22, 23 (left and right), and 40 (left).
Pete Krumhardt: pages 36–37, 44 (bottom left), 45, 49 (top right), 90, 91, and 94–95.
Scott Little: pages 68, 95 (top and bottom), 96, 97 (right), 99, 100, and 101.
Andy Lyons: pages 56, 98 (top), 102, and 103.
Barbara Martin: page 15 (top).
Blaine Moats: page 55 (bottom left and bottom right).
John Noltner: page 5.
Michael Partenio: pages 7, 8 (left and right), 13, 88–89, and 92 (bottom).
Cameron Sadeghpour: pages 17 (ornaments #1–7), 18, 19, 39 (left and right), 51 (left and right), 53, 59, 60 (top and bottom), 62 (bottom), 63 (top and bottom), 64–65, 78, 79 (top and bottom), 80, 81, 82, and 83 (top and bottom).
Greg Scheidemann: pages 11 (top and bottom), 15 (bottom), 20, 21 (left), 44 (top), 60 (left and right), 66, 67, 69, 70, 71 (top and bottom), 72 (left and right), 85, and 87.
Bill Stites: page 52 (right).
Jay Wilde: pages 12, 26 (top right, bottom left, and bottom right), 58 (all), 76, and 77 (top and bottom).